T0256703

Concurrency in Go
Tools and Techniques for Developers

Katherine Cox-Buday

Beijing · Boston · Farnham · Sebastopol · Tokyo

Concurrency in Go

by Katherine Cox-Buday

Printed in the United States of America.

Published by O'Reilly Media, Inc., 1005 Gravenstein Highway North, Sebastopol, CA 95472.

O'Reilly books may be purchased for educational, business, or sales promotional use. Online editions are also available for most titles (*http://oreilly.com/safari*). For more information, contact our corporate/institutional sales department: 800-998-9938 or *corporate@oreilly.com*.

Editor: Dawn Schanafelt	**Indexer:** Judy McConville
Production Editor: Nicholas Adams	**Interior Designer:** David Futato
Copyeditor: Kim Cofer	**Cover Designer:** Karen Montgomery
Proofreader: Sonia Saruba	**Illustrator:** Rebecca Demarest

August 2017:   First Edition

Revision History for the First Edition
2017-07-18:   First Release

See *http://oreilly.com/catalog/errata.csp?isbn=9781491941195* for release details.

978-1-491-94119-5

[LSI]

For L. and N. whose sacrifice made this book possible. Of everything in my life, you are the best. I love you.

Table of Contents

Preface

Hey, welcome to *Concurrency in Go*! I'm delighted that you've picked up this book and excited to join you in exploring the topic of concurrency in Go over the next six chapters!

Go is a wonderful language. When it was first announced and birthed into the world, I remember exploring it with great interest: it was terse, compiled incredibly fast, performed well, supported duck typing, and—to my delight—I found working with its concurrency primitives to be intuitive. The first time I used the go keyword to create a goroutine (something we'll cover, I promise!) I got this silly grin on my face. I had worked with concurrency in several languages, but I had never worked in a language that made concurrency so easy (which is not to say they don't exist; I just hadn't used any). I had found my way to Go.

Over the years I moved from writing personal scripts in Go, to personal projects, until I found myself working on a many-hundreds-of-thousands-of-lines project professionally. Along the way the community was growing with the language, and we were collectively discovering best practices for working with concurrency in Go. A few people gave talks on patterns they had discovered. But there still weren't many comprehensive guides on how to wield concurrency in Go in the community.

It was with this in mind that I set out to write this book. I wanted the community to have access to high-quality and comprehensive information about concurrency in Go: how to use it, best practices and patterns for incorporating it into your systems, and how it all works under the covers. I have done my best to strike a balance between these concerns.

I hope this book proves useful!

Who Should Read This Book

This book is meant for developers who have some experience with Go; I make no attempt to explain the basic syntax of the language. Knowledge of how concurrency is presented in other languages is useful, but not necessary.

By the end of this book we will have discussed the entire stack of Go concurrency concerns: common concurrency pitfalls, motivation behind the design of Go's concurrency, the basic syntax of Go's concurrency primitives, common concurrency patterns, patterns of patterns, and various tooling that will help you along the way.

Because of the breadth of topics we'll cover, this book will be useful to various cross-sections of people. The next section will help you navigate this book depending on what needs you have.

Navigating This Book

When I read technical books, I usually hop around to the areas that pique my interest. Or, if I'm trying to ramp up on a new technology for work, I frantically skim for the bits that are immediately relevant to my work. Whatever your use case is, here's a roadmap for the book with the hopes that it help guide you to where you need to be!

Chapter 1, An Introduction to Concurrency
> This chapter will give you a broad historical perspective on why concurrency is an important concept, and also discuss some of the fundamental problems that make concurrency difficult to get correct. It also briefly touches on how Go helps ease some of this burden.
>
> If you have a working knowledge of concurrency or just want to get to the technical aspects of how to use Go's concurrency primitives, it's safe to skip this chapter.

Chapter 2, Modeling Your Code: Communicating Sequential Processes
> This chapter deals with some of the motivational factors that contributed to Go's design. This will help give you some context for conversations with others in the Go community and help to frame your understanding of why things work the way they do in the language.

Chapter 3, Go's Concurrency Building Blocks
> Here we'll start to dig into the syntax of Go's concurrency primitives. We'll also cover the sync package, which is responsible for handling Go's memory access synchronization. If you haven't used concurrency within Go before and are looking to hop right in, this is the place to start.

Interspersed with the basics of writing concurrent code in Go are comparisons of concepts to other languages and concurrency models. Strictly speaking, it's not necessary to understand these things, but these concepts help you to achieve a complete understanding on concurrency in Go.

Chapter 4, Concurrency Patterns in Go

In this chapter, we begin to look at how Go's concurrency primitives are composed together to form useful patterns. These patterns will both help us solve problems and avoid issues that can come up when combining concurrency primitives.

If you've already been writing some concurrent code in Go, this chapter should still prove useful.

Chapter 5, Concurrency at Scale

In this chapter, we take the patterns we have learned and compose these into larger patterns commonly employed in larger programs, services, and distributed systems.

Chapter 6, Goroutines and the Go Runtime

This chapter describes how the Go runtime handles scheduling goroutines. This is for those of you who want to understand the internals of Go's runtime.

Appendix

The appendix simply enumerates various tools and commands that can help make writing and debugging concurrent programs easier.

Online Resources

Go has a very active and passionate community! For those newer to Go, take heart, it will be easy to find friendly, helpful people to guide you along on your path to Go. Here are a few of my favorite community-oriented resources for reading, getting help, and interacting with your fellow gophers:

- *https://golang.org/*
- *https://golang.org/play*
- *https://go.googlesource.com/go*
- *https://groups.google.com/group/golang-nuts*
- *https://github.com/golang/go/wiki*

Conventions Used in This Book

The following typographical conventions are used in this book:

Italic
> Indicates new terms, URLs, email addresses, filenames, and file extensions.

`Constant width`
> Used for program listings, as well as within paragraphs to refer to program elements such as variable or function names, databases, data types, environment variables, statements, and keywords.

`Constant width bold`
> Shows commands or other text that should be typed literally by the user.

`Constant width italic`
> Shows text that should be replaced with user-supplied values or by values determined by context.

> This icon signifies a tip, suggestion, or general note.

> This icon indicates a warning or caution.

Using Code Examples

All of the code contained in this book can be found on the landing page for the book, *http://katherine.cox-buday.com/concurrency-in-go*. It is released under the MIT license and may be used under those terms.

O'Reilly Safari

Safari (formerly Safari Books Online) is a membership-based training and reference platform for enterprise, government, educators, and individuals.

Members have access to thousands of books, training videos, Learning Paths, interactive tutorials, and curated playlists from over 250 publishers, including O'Reilly Media, Harvard Business Review, Prentice Hall Professional, Addison-Wesley Professional, Microsoft Press, Sams, Que, Peachpit Press, Adobe, Focal Press, Cisco Press, John Wiley & Sons, Syngress, Morgan Kaufmann, IBM Redbooks, Packt, Adobe Press, FT Press, Apress, Manning, New Riders, McGraw-Hill, Jones & Bartlett, and Course Technology, among others.

For more information, please visit *http://oreilly.com/safari*.

How to Contact Us

Please address comments and questions concerning this book to the publisher:

O'Reilly Media, Inc.
1005 Gravenstein Highway North
Sebastopol, CA 95472
800-998-9938 (in the United States or Canada)
707-829-0515 (international or local)
707-829-0104 (fax)

We have a web page for this book, where we list errata, examples, and any additional information. You can access this page at *http://bit.ly/concurrency-in-go*.

To comment or ask technical questions about this book, send email to *bookquestions@oreilly.com*.

For more information about our books, courses, conferences, and news, see our website at *http://www.oreilly.com*.

Find us on Facebook: *http://facebook.com/oreilly*

Follow us on Twitter: *http://twitter.com/oreillymedia*

Watch us on YouTube: *http://www.youtube.com/oreillymedia*

Acknowledgments

Writing a book is a daunting and challenging task. What you have before you would not have been possible without a team of people supporting me, reviewing things, writing tools, and answering questions. I am deeply grateful to everyone who helped, and they have my sincerest thanks. We did this together!

One swallow does not a summer make...
    —Proverb

- Alan Donovan, who helped with the original proposal and also helped set me on my way.

- Andrew Wilkins, who I had the great fortune of working with at Canonical. His insight, professionalism, and intelligence influenced this book, and his reviews made it better.

- Ara Pulido, who helped me see this book through a new gopher's eyes.

- Dawn Schanafelt, my editor, who played a large part in making this book read as clearly as possible. I especially appreciate her (and O'Reilly's) patience while life placed a few difficulties on my path while writing this book.

- Francesc Campoy, who helped ensure I always kept newer gophers in mind.

- Ivan Daniluk, whose attention to detail and interest in concurrency helped ensure this is a comprehensive and useful book.

- Yasushi Shoji, who wrote `org-asciidoc`, a tool that I used to export AsciiDoc artifacts from Org mode. He didn't know he was helping to write a book, but he was always very responsive to bug reports and questions!

- The maintainers of Go: thank you for your dedication.

- The maintainers of Org mode, the GNU Emacs mode with which this book is written. My entire life is in org; seriously, thanks all.

- The maintainers of GNU Emacs, the text editor I wrote this book in. I cannot think of a tool that has served as more of a lever in my life.

- The St. Louis public libraries where most of this book was written.

CHAPTER 1

An Introduction to Concurrency

Concurrency is an interesting word because it means different things to different people in our field. In addition to "concurrency," you may have heard the words, "asynchronous," "parallel," or "threaded" bandied about. Some people take these words to mean the same thing, and other people very specifically delineate between each of those words. If we're to spend an entire book's worth of time discussing concurrency, it would be beneficial to first spend some time discussing what we mean when we say "concurrency."

We'll spend some time on the philosophy of concurrency in Chapter 2, but for now let's adopt a practical definition that will serve as the foundation of our understanding.

When most people use the word "concurrent," they're usually referring to a process that occurs simultaneously with one or more processes. It is also usually implied that all of these processes are making progress at about the same time. Under this definition, an easy way to think about this are people. You are currently reading this sentence while others in the world are simultaneously living their lives. They are existing *concurrently* to you.

Concurrency is a broad topic in computer science, and from this definition spring all kinds of topics: theory, approaches to modeling concurrency, correctness of logic, practical issues—even theoretical physics! We'll touch on some of the ancillary topics throughout the book, but we'll mostly stick to the practical issues that involve understanding concurrency within the context of Go, specifically: how Go chooses to model concurrency, what issues arise from this model, and how we can compose primitives within this model to solve problems.

In this chapter, we'll take a broad look at some of the reasons concurrency became such an important topic in computer science, why concurrency is difficult and warrants careful study, and—most importantly—the idea that despite these challenges, Go can make programs clearer and faster by using its concurrency primitives.

As with most paths toward understanding, we'll begin with a bit of history. Let's first take a look at how concurrency became such an important topic.

Moore's Law, Web Scale, and the Mess We're In

In 1965, Gordon Moore wrote a three-page paper that described both the consolidation of the electronics market toward integrated circuits, and the doubling of the number of components in an integrated circuit every year for at least a decade. In 1975, he revised this prediction to state that the number of components on an integrated circuit would double every two years. This prediction more or less held true until just recently—around 2012.

Several companies foresaw this slowdown in the rate Moore's law predicted and began to investigate alternative ways to increase computing power. As the saying goes, necessity is the mother of innovation, and so it was in this way that multicore processors were born.

This looked like a clever way to solve the bounding problems of Moore's law, but computer scientists soon found themselves facing down the limits of another law: Amdahl's law, named after computer architect Gene Amdahl.

Amdahl's law describes a way in which to model the potential performance gains from implementing the solution to a problem in a parallel manner. Simply put, it states that the gains are bounded by how much of the program must be written in a sequential manner.

For example, imagine you were writing a program that was largely GUI based: a user is presented with an interface, clicks on some buttons, and stuff happens. This type of program is bounded by one very large sequential portion of the pipeline: human interaction. No matter how many cores you make available to this program, it will always be bounded by how quickly the user can interact with the interface.

Now consider a different example, calculating digits of pi. Thanks to a class of algorithms called spigot algorithms (*https://en.wikipedia.org/wiki/Spigot_algorithm*), this problem is called *embarrassingly parallel*, which—despite sounding made up—is a technical term which means that it can easily be divided into parallel tasks. In this case, significant gains can be made by making more cores available to your program, and your new problem becomes how to combine and store the results.

Amdahl's law helps us understand the difference between these two problems, and can help us decide whether parallelization is the right way to address performance concerns in our system.

For problems that are embarrassingly parallel, it is recommended that you write your application so that it can *scale horizontally*. This means that you can take instances of your program, run it on more CPUs, or machines, and this will cause the runtime of the system to improve. Embarrassingly parallel problems fit this model so well because it's very easy to structure your program in such a way that you can send chunks of a problem to different instances of your application.

Scaling horizontally became much easier in the early 2000s when a new paradigm began to take hold: *cloud computing*. Although there are indications that the phrase had been used as early as the 1970s, the early 2000s are when the idea really took root in the zeitgeist. Cloud computing implied a new kind of scale and approach to application deployments and horizontal scaling. Instead of machines that you carefully curated, installed software on, and maintained, cloud computing implied access to vast pools of resources that were provisioned into machines for workloads on-demand. Machines became something that were almost ephemeral, and provisioned with characteristics specifically suited to the programs they would run. Usually (but not always) these resource pools were hosted in data centers owned by other companies.

This change encouraged a new kind of thinking. Suddenly, developers had relatively cheap access to vast amounts of computing power that they could use to solve large problems. Solutions could now trivially span many machines and even global regions. Cloud computing made possible a whole new set of solutions to problems that were previously only solvable by tech giants.

But cloud computing also presented many new challenges. Provisioning these resources, communicating between machine instances, and aggregating and storing the results all became problems to solve. But among the most difficult was figuring out how to model code concurrently. The fact that pieces of your solution could be running on disparate machines exacerbated some of the issues commonly faced when modeling a problem concurrently. Successfully solving these issues soon led to a new type of brand for software, *web scale*.

If software was web scale, among other things, you could expect that it would be embarrassingly parallel; that is, web scale software is usually expected to be able to handle hundreds of thousands (or more) of simultaneous workloads by adding more instances of the application. This enabled all kinds of properties like rolling upgrades, elastic horizontally scalable architecture, and geographic distribution. It also introduced new levels of complexity both in comprehension and fault tolerance.

And so it is in this world of multiple cores, cloud computing, web scale, and problems that may or may not be parallelizable that we find the modern developer, maybe a bit overwhelmed. The proverbial buck has been passed to us, and we are expected to rise to the challenge of solving problems within the confines of the hardware we've been handed. In 2005, Herb Sutter authored an article for *Dr. Dobb's*, titled, "The free lunch is over: A fundamental turn toward concurrency in software" (*http://www.gotw.ca/publications/concurrency-ddj.htm*). The title is apt, and the article prescient. Toward the end, Sutter states, "We desperately need a higher-level programming model for concurrency than languages offer today."

To know why Sutter used such strong language, we have to look at why concurrency is so hard to get right.

Why Is Concurrency Hard?

Concurrent code is notoriously difficult to get right. It usually takes a few iterations to get it working as expected, and even then it's not uncommon for bugs to exist in code for years before some change in timing (heavier disk utilization, more users logged into the system, etc.) causes a previously undiscovered bug to rear its head. Indeed, for this very book, I've gotten as many eyes as possbile on the code to try and mitigate this.

Fortunately *everyone* runs into the same issues when working with concurrent code. Because of this, computer scientists have been able to label the common issues, which allows us to discuss how they arise, why, and how to solve them.

So let's get started. Following are some of the most common issues that make working with concurrent code both frustrating and interesting.

Race Conditions

A race condition occurs when two or more operations must execute in the correct order, but the program has not been written so that this order is guaranteed to be maintained.

Most of the time, this shows up in what's called a *data race*, where one concurrent operation attempts to read a variable while at some undetermined time another concurrent operation is attempting to write to the same variable.

Here's a basic example:

```
1 var data int
2 go func() {  ❶
3     data++
4 }()
5 if data == 0 {
6     fmt.Printf("the value is %v.\n", data)
7 }
```

❶ In Go, you can use the go keyword to run a function concurrently. Doing so creates what's called a *goroutine*. We'll discuss this in detail in the section, "Goroutines" on page 37.

Here, lines 3 and 5 are both trying to access the variable data, but there is no guarantee what order this might happen in. There are three possible outcomes to running this code:

- Nothing is printed. In this case, line 3 was executed before line 5.
- "the value is 0" is printed. In this case, lines 5 and 6 were executed before line 3.
- "the value is 1" is printed. In this case, line 5 was executed before line 3, but line 3 was executed before line 6.

As you can see, just a few lines of incorrect code can introduce tremendous variability into your program.

Most of the time, data races are introduced because the developers are thinking about the problem sequentially. They assume that because a line of code falls before another that it will run first. They assume the goroutine above will be scheduled and execute before the data variable is read in the if statement.

When writing concurrent code, you have to meticulously iterate through the possible scenarios. Unless you're utilizing some of the techniques we'll cover later in the book, you have no guarantees that your code will run in the order it's listed in the source-code. I sometimes find it helpful to imagine a large period of time passing between operations. Imagine an hour passes between the time when the goroutine is invoked, and when it is run. How would the rest of the program behave? What if it took an hour between the goroutine executing successfully and the program reaching the if statement? Thinking in this manner helps me because to a computer, the scale may be different, but the relative time differentials are more or less the same.

Indeed, some developers fall into the trap of sprinkling sleeps throughout their code exactly because it seems to solve their concurrency problems. Let's try that in the preceding program:

```
1 var data int
2 go func() { data++ }()
3 time.Sleep(1*time.Second) // This is bad!
4 if data == 0 {
5     fmt.Printf("the value is %v.\n" data)
6 }
```

Have we solved our data race? No. In fact, it's still possible for all three outcomes to arise from this program, just increasingly *unlikely*. The longer we sleep in between invoking our goroutine and checking the value of data, the closer our program gets to achieving correctness—but this probability asymptotically approaches logical correctness; it will never be logically correct.

In addition to this, we've now introduced an inefficiency into our algorithm. We now have to sleep for one second to make it more likely we won't see our data race. If we utilized the correct tools, we might not have to wait at all, or the wait could be only a microsecond.

The takeaway here is that you should always target logical correctness. Introducing sleeps into your code can be a handy way to debug concurrent programs, but they are not a solution.

Race conditions are one of the most insidious types of concurrency bugs because they may not show up until years after the code has been placed into production. They are usually precipitated by a change in the environment the code is executing in, or an unprecedented occurrence. In these cases, the code seems to be behaving correctly, but in reality, there's just a very high chance that the operations will be executed in order. Sooner or later, the program will have an unintended consequence.

Atomicity

When something is considered atomic, or to have the property of atomicity, this means that within the context that it is operating, it is indivisible, or uninterruptible.

So what does that really mean, and why is this important to know when working with concurrent code?

The first thing that's very important is the word "context." Something may be atomic in one context, but not another. Operations that are atomic within the context of your process may not be atomic in the context of the operating system; operations that are atomic within the context of the operating system may not be atomic within the context of your machine; and operations that are atomic within the context of your machine may not be atomic within the context of your application. In other words, the atomicity of an operation can change depending on the currently defined scope. This fact can work both for and against you!

When thinking about atomicity, very often the first thing you need to do is to define the context, or scope, the operation will be considered to be atomic in. Everything follows from this.

Fun Fact

In 2006, the gaming company Blizzard successfully sued MDY Industries for $6,000,000 USD for making a program called "Glider," which would automatically play their game, World of Warcraft, without user intervention. These types of programs are commonly referred to as "bots" (short for robots).

At the time, World of Warcraft had an anti-cheating program called "Warden," which would run anytime you played the game. Among other things, Warden would scan the memory of the host machine and run a heuristic to look for programs that appeared to be used for cheating.

Glider successfully avoided this check by taking advantage of the concept of atomic context. Warden considered scanning the memory on the machine as an atomic operation, but Glider utilized hardware interrupts to hide itself before this scanning started! Warden's scan of memory was atomic within the context of the process, but not within the context of the operating system.

Now let's look at the terms "indivisible" and "uninterruptible." These terms mean that within the context you've defined, something that is atomic will happen in its entirety without anything happening in that context simultaneously. That's still a mouthful, so let's look at an example:

```
i++
```

This is about as simple an example as anyone can contrive, and yet it easily demonstrates the concept of atomicity. It may *look* atomic, but a brief analysis reveals several operations:

- Retrieve the value of i.
- Increment the value of i.
- Store the value of i.

While each of these operations alone is atomic, the combination of the three may not be, depending on your context. This reveals an interesting property of atomic operations: combining them does not necessarily produce a larger atomic operation. Making the operation atomic is dependent on which context you'd like it to be atomic within. If your context is a program with no concurrent processes, then this code is atomic within that context. If your context is a goroutine that doesn't expose i to other goroutines, then this code is atomic.

So why do we care? Atomicity is important because if something is atomic, implicitly it is safe within concurrent contexts. This allows us to compose logically correct programs, and—as we'll later see—can even serve as a way to optimize concurrent programs.

Most statements are not atomic, let alone functions, methods, and programs. If atomicity is the key to composing logically correct programs, and most statements aren't atomic, how do we reconcile these two statements? We'll go into more depth later, but in short we can force atomicity by employing various techniques. The art then becomes determining which areas of your code need to be atomic, and at what level of granularity. We discuss some of these challenges in the next section.

Memory Access Synchronization

Let's say we have a data race: two concurrent processes are attempting to access the same area of memory, and the way they are accessing the memory is not atomic. Our previous example of a simple data race will do nicely with a few modifications:

```
var data int
go func() { data++}()
if data == 0 {
    fmt.Println("the value is 0.")
} else {
    fmt.Printf("the value is %v.\n", data)
}
```

We've added an `else` clause here so that regardless of the value of `data` we'll always get some output. Remember that as it is written, there is a data race and the output of the program will be completely nondeterministic.

In fact, there's a name for a section of your program that needs exclusive access to a shared resource. This is called a *critical section*. In this example, we have three critical sections:

- Our goroutine, which is incrementing the `data` variables.
- Our `if` statement, which checks whether the value of `data` is 0.
- Our `fmt.Printf` statement, which retrieves the value of `data` for output.

There are various ways to guard your program's critical sections, and Go has some better ideas on how to deal with this, but one way to solve this problem is to synchronize access to the memory between your critical sections. Let's see what that looks like.

The following code is not idiomatic Go (and I don't suggest you attempt to solve your data race problems like this), but it very simply demonstrates memory access synchronization. If any of the types, functions, or methods in this example are foreign to you, that's OK. Focus on the concept of synchronizing access to the memory by following the callouts.

```
var memoryAccess sync.Mutex ❶
var value int
go func() {
    memoryAccess.Lock() ❷
    value++
    memoryAccess.Unlock() ❸
}()

memoryAccess.Lock() ❹
if value == 0 {
    fmt.Printf("the value is %v.\n", value)
```

```
    } else {
        fmt.Printf("the value is %v.\n", value)
    }
    memoryAccess.Unlock()  ❺
```

❶ Here we add a variable that will allow our code to synchronize access to the data variable's memory. We'll go over the sync.Mutex type in detail in "The sync Package" on page 47.

❷ Here we declare that until we declare otherwise, our goroutine should have exclusive access to this memory.

❸ Here we declare that the goroutine is done with this memory.

❹ Here we once again declare that the following conditional statements should have exclusive access to the data variable's memory.

❺ Here we declare we're once again done with this memory.

In this example we've created a convention for developers to follow. Anytime developers want to access the data variable's memory, they must first call Lock, and when they're finished they must call Unlock. Code between those two statements can then assume it has exclusive access to data; we have successfully *synchronized* access to the memory. Also note that if developers don't follow this convention, we have no guarantee of exclusive access! We'll return to this idea in the section "Confinement" on page 85.

You may have noticed that while we have solved our data race, we haven't actually solved our race condition! The order of operations in this program is still nondeterministic; we've just narrowed the scope of the nondeterminism a bit. In this example, either the goroutine will execute first, or both our if and else blocks will. We still don't know which will occur first in any given execution of this program. Later, we'll explore the tools to solve this kind of issue properly.

On its face this seems pretty simple: if you find you have critical sections, add points to synchronize access to the memory! Easy, right? Well…sort of.

It is true that you can solve some problems by synchronizing access to the memory, but as we just saw, it doesn't automatically solve data races or logical correctness. Further, it can also create maintenance and performance problems.

Note that earlier we mentioned that we had created a *convention* for declaring we needed exclusive access to some memory. Conventions are great, but they're also easy to ignore—especially in software engineering where the demands of business sometimes outweigh prudence. By synchronizing access to the memory in this manner, you are counting on all other developers to follow the same convention now and into the future. That's a pretty tall order. Thankfully, later in this book we'll also look at some ways we can help our colleagues be more successful.

Synchronizing access to the memory in this manner also has performance ramifications. We'll save the details for later when we examine the sync package in the section "The sync Package" on page 47, but the calls to Lock you see can make our program *slow*. Every time we perform one of these operations, our program pauses for a period of time. This brings up two questions:

- Are my critical sections entered and exited repeatedly?
- What size should my critical sections be?

Answering these two questions in the context of your program is an art, and this adds to the difficulty in synchronizing access to the memory.

Synchronizing access to the memory also shares some problems with other techniques of modeling concurrent problems, and we'll discuss those in the next section.

Deadlocks, Livelocks, and Starvation

The previous sections have all been about discussing program correctness in that if these issues are managed correctly, your program will never give an incorrect answer. Unfortunately, even if you successfully handle these classes of issues, there is another class of issues to contend with: deadlocks, livelocks, and starvation. These issues all concern ensuring your program has something useful to do at all times. If not handled properly, your program could enter a state in which it will stop functioning altogether.

Deadlock

A deadlocked program is one in which all concurrent processes are waiting on one another. In this state, the program will never recover without outside intervention.

If that sounds grim, it's because it is! The Go runtime attempts to do its part and will detect some deadlocks (all goroutines must be blocked, or "asleep"[1]), but this doesn't do much to help you prevent deadlocks.

To help solidify what a deadlock is, let's first look at an example. Again, it's safe to ignore any types, functions, methods, or packages you don't know and just follow the code callouts.

```
type value struct {
    mu    sync.Mutex
```

---

1 There is an accepted proposal to allow the runtime to detect partial deadlocks, but it has not been implemented. For more information, see *https://github.com/golang/go/issues/13759*.

```
    value int
}

var wg sync.WaitGroup
printSum := func(v1, v2 *value) {
    defer wg.Done()
    v1.mu.Lock() ❶
    defer v1.mu.Unlock() ❷

    time.Sleep(2*time.Second) ❸
    v2.mu.Lock()
    defer v2.mu.Unlock()

    fmt.Printf("sum=%v\n", v1.value + v2.value)
}

var a, b value
wg.Add(2)
go printSum(&a, &b)
go printSum(&b, &a)
wg.Wait()
```

❶   Here we attempt to enter the critical section for the incoming value.

❷   Here we use the `defer` statement to exit the critical section before `printSum` returns.

❸   Here we sleep for a period of time to simulate work (and trigger a deadlock).

If you were to try and run this code, you'd probably see:

```
fatal error: all goroutines are asleep - deadlock!
```

Why? If you look carefully, you'll see a timing issue in this code. Following is a graphical representation of what's going on. The boxes represent functions, the horizontal lines calls to these functions, and the vertical bars lifetimes of the function at the head of the graphic (Figure 1-1).

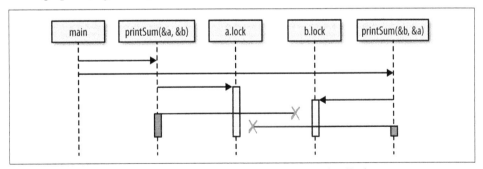

Figure 1-1. Demonstration of a timing issue giving rise to a deadlock

Essentially, we have created two gears that cannot turn together: our first call to `print Sum` locks a and then attempts to lock b, but in the meantime our second call to `print Sum` has locked b and has attempted to lock a. Both goroutines wait infinitely on each other.

Irony

To keep this example simple, I use a `time.Sleep` to trigger the deadlock. However, this introduces a race condition! Can you find it?

A logically "perfect" deadlock would require correct synchronization.[2]

It seems pretty obvious why this deadlock is occurring when we lay it out graphically like that, but we would benefit from a more rigorous definition. It turns out there are a few conditions that must be present for deadlocks to arise, and in 1971, Edgar Coffman enumerated these conditions in a paper (*http://bit.ly/CoffmanDeadlocks*). The conditions are now known as the *Coffman Conditions* and are the basis for techniques that help detect, prevent, and correct deadlocks.

The Coffman Conditions are as follows:

Mutual Exclusion
  A concurrent process holds exclusive rights to a resource at any one time.

Wait For Condition
  A concurrent process must simultaneously hold a resource and be waiting for an additional resource.

No Preemption
  A resource held by a concurrent process can only be released by that process, so it fulfills this condition.

Circular Wait
  A concurrent process (P1) must be waiting on a chain of other concurrent processes (P2), which are in turn waiting on it (P1), so it fulfills this final condition too.

---

2 We actually have no guarantee what order the goroutines will run in, or how long it will take them to start. It's plausible, although unlikely, that one goroutine could acquire and release both locks before the other begins, thus avoiding the deadlock!

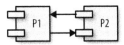

Let's examine our contrived program and determine if it meets all four conditions:

1. The `printSum` function does require exclusive rights to both a and b, so it fulfills this condition.

2. Because `printSum` holds either a or b and is waiting on the other, it fulfills this condition.

3. We haven't given any way for our goroutines to be preempted.

4. Our first invocation of `printSum` is waiting on our second invocation, and vice versa.

Yep, we definitely have a deadlock on our hands.

These laws allow us to *prevent* deadlocks too. If we ensure that at least one of these conditions is not true, we can prevent deadlocks from occurring. Unfortunately, in practice these conditions can be hard to reason about, and therefore difficult to prevent. The web is strewn with questions from developers like you and me wondering why a snippet of code is deadlocking. Usually it's pretty obvious once someone points it out, but often it requires another set of eyes. We'll talk about why this is in the section "Determining Concurrency Safety" on page 18.

Livelock

Livelocks are programs that are actively performing concurrent operations, but these operations do nothing to move the state of the program forward.

Have you ever been in a hallway walking toward another person? She moves to one side to let you pass, but you've just done the same. So you move to the other side, but she's also done the same. Imagine this going on forever, and you understand livelocks.

Let's actually write some code that will help demonstrate this scenario. First, we'll set up a few helper functions that will simplify the example. In order to have a working example, the code here utilizes several topics we haven't yet covered. I don't advise attempting to understand it in any detail until you have a firm grasp on the `sync` package. Instead, I recommend following the code callouts to understand the highlights, and then turning your attention to the second code block, which contains the heart of the example.

```
cadence := sync.NewCond(&sync.Mutex{})
go func() {
    for range time.Tick(1*time.Millisecond) {
```

```
        cadence.Broadcast()
    }
}()

takeStep := func() {
    cadence.L.Lock()
    cadence.Wait()
    cadence.L.Unlock()
}

tryDir := func(dirName string, dir *int32, out *bytes.Buffer) bool { ❶
    fmt.Fprintf(out, " %v", dirName)
    atomic.AddInt32(dir, 1) ❷
    takeStep() ❸
    if atomic.LoadInt32(dir) == 1 {
        fmt.Fprint(out, ". Success!")
        return true
    }
    takeStep()
    atomic.AddInt32(dir, -1) ❹
    return false
}

var left, right int32
tryLeft := func(out *bytes.Buffer) bool { return tryDir("left", &left, out) }
tryRight := func(out *bytes.Buffer) bool { return tryDir("right", &right, out) }
```

❶ tryDir allows a person to attempt to move in a direction and returns whether or not they were successful. Each direction is represented as a count of the number of people trying to move in that direction, dir.

❷ First, we declare our intention to move in a direction by incrementing that direction by one. We'll discuss the atomic package in detail in Chapter 3. For now, all you need to know is that this package's operations are atomic.

❸ For the example to demonstrate a livelock, each person must move at the same rate of speed, or cadence. takeStep simulates a constant cadence between all parties.

❹ Here the person realizes they cannot go in this direction and gives up. We indicate this by decrementing that direction by one.

```
walk := func(walking *sync.WaitGroup, name string) {
    var out bytes.Buffer
    defer func() { fmt.Println(out.String()) }()
    defer walking.Done()
    fmt.Fprintf(&out, "%v is trying to scoot:", name)
    for i := 0; i < 5; i++ { ❶
        if tryLeft(&out) || tryRight(&out) { ❷
```

```
            return
        }
    }
    fmt.Fprintf(&out, "\n%v tosses her hands up in exasperation!", name)
}

var peopleInHallway sync.WaitGroup ❸
peopleInHallway.Add(2)
go walk(&peopleInHallway, "Alice")
go walk(&peopleInHallway, "Barbara")
peopleInHallway.Wait()
```

❶ I placed an artificial limit on the number of attempts so that this program would end. In a program that has a livelock, there may be no such limit, which is why it's a problem!

❷ First, the person will attempt to step left, and if that fails, they will attempt to step right.

❸ This variable provides a way for the program to wait until both people are either able to pass one another, or give up.

This produces the following output:

```
Alice is trying to scoot: left right left right left right left right left right
Alice tosses her hands up in exasperation!
Barbara is trying to scoot: left right left right left right left right
left right
Barbara tosses her hands up in exasperation!
```

You can see that Alice and Barbara continue getting in each other's way before finally giving up.

This example demonstrates a very common reason livelocks are written: two or more concurrent processes attempting to prevent a deadlock without coordination. If the people in the hallway had agreed with one another that only one person would move, there would be no livelock: one person would stand still, the other would move to the other side, and they'd continue walking.

In my opinion, livelocks are more difficult to spot than deadlocks simply because it can appear as if the program is doing work. If a livelocked program were running on your machine and you took a look at the CPU utilization to determine if it was doing anything, you might think it was. Depending on the livelock, it might even be emitting other signals that would make you think it was doing work. And yet all the while, your program would be playing an eternal game of hallway-shuffle.

Livelocks are a subset of a larger set of problems called *starvation*. We'll look at that next.

Starvation

Starvation is any situation where a concurrent process cannot get all the resources it needs to perform work.

When we discussed livelocks, the resource each goroutine was starved of was a shared lock. Livelocks warrant discussion separate from starvation because in a live-lock, all the concurrent processes are starved equally, and *no* work is accomplished. More broadly, starvation usually implies that there are one or more greedy concurrent process that are unfairly preventing one or more concurrent processes from accomplishing work as efficiently as possible, or maybe at all.

Here's an example of a program with a greedy goroutine and a polite goroutine:

```
var wg sync.WaitGroup
var sharedLock sync.Mutex
const runtime = 1*time.Second

greedyWorker := func() {
    defer wg.Done()

    var count int
    for begin := time.Now(); time.Since(begin) <= runtime; {
        sharedLock.Lock()
        time.Sleep(3*time.Nanosecond)
        sharedLock.Unlock()
        count++
    }

    fmt.Printf("Greedy worker was able to execute %v work loops\n", count)
}

politeWorker := func() {
    defer wg.Done()

    var count int
    for begin := time.Now(); time.Since(begin) <= runtime; {
        sharedLock.Lock()
        time.Sleep(1*time.Nanosecond)
        sharedLock.Unlock()

        sharedLock.Lock()
        time.Sleep(1*time.Nanosecond)
        sharedLock.Unlock()

        sharedLock.Lock()
        time.Sleep(1*time.Nanosecond)
        sharedLock.Unlock()

        count++
    }
```

```
        fmt.Printf("Polite worker was able to execute %v work loops.\n", count)
    }

    wg.Add(2)
    go greedyWorker()
    go politeWorker()

    wg.Wait()
```

This produces:

```
    Polite worker was able to execute 289777 work loops.
    Greedy worker was able to execute 471287 work loops
```

The greedy worker greedily holds onto the shared lock for the entirety of its work loop, whereas the polite worker attempts to only lock when it needs to. Both workers do the same amount of simulated work (sleeping for three nanoseconds), but as you can see in the same amount of time, the greedy worker got almost *twice* the amount of work done!

If we assume both workers have the same-sized critical section, rather than concluding that the greedy worker's algorithm is more efficient (or that the calls to Lock and Unlock are slow—they aren't), we instead conclude that the greedy worker has unnecessarily expanded its hold on the shared lock beyond its critical section and is preventing (via starvation) the polite worker's goroutine from performing work efficiently.

Note our technique here for identifying the starvation: a metric. Starvation makes for a good argument for recording and sampling metrics. One of the ways you can detect and solve starvation is by logging when work is accomplished, and then determining if your rate of work is as high as you expect it.

Finding a Balance

It is worth mentioning that the previous code example can also serve as an example of the performance ramifications of memory access synchronization. Because synchronizing access to the memory is expensive, it might be advantageous to broaden our lock beyond our critical sections. On the other hand, by doing so—as we saw—we run the risk of starving other concurrent processes.

If you utilize memory access synchronization, you'll have to find a balance between preferring coarse-grained synchronization for performance, and fine-grained synchronization for fairness. When it comes time to performance tune your application, to start with, I highly recommend you constrain memory access synchronization only to critical sections; if the synchronization becomes a performance problem, you can always broaden the scope. It's much harder to go the other way.

So starvation can cause your program to behave inefficiently or incorrectly. The prior example demonstrates an inefficiency, but if you have a concurrent process that is so greedy as to *completely* prevent another concurrent process from accomplishing work, you have a larger problem on your hands.

We should also consider the case where the starvation is coming from outside the Go process. Keep in mind that starvation can also apply to CPU, memory, file handles, database connections: any resource that must be shared is a candidate for starvation.

Determining Concurrency Safety

Finally, we come to the most difficult aspect of developing concurrent code, the thing that underlies all the other problems: people. Behind every line of code is at least one person.

As we've discovered, concurrent code is difficult for myriad reasons. If you're a developer and you're trying to wrangle all of these problems as you introduce new functionality, or fix bugs in your program, it can be really difficult to determine the right thing to do.

If you're starting with a blank slate and need to build up a sensible way to model your problem space and concurrency is involved, it can be difficult to find the right level of abstraction. How do you expose the concurrency to callers? What techniques do you use to create a solution that is both easy to use and modify? What is the right *level* of concurrency for this problem? Although there are ways to think about these problems in structured ways, it remains an art.

As a developer interfacing with *existing* code, it's not always obvious what code is utilizing concurrency, and how to utilize the code safely. Take this function signature:

```
// CalculatePi calculates digits of Pi between the begin and end
// place.
func CalculatePi(begin, end int64, pi *Pi)
```

Calculating pi with a large precision is something that is best done concurrently, but this example raises a lot of questions:

- How do I do so with this function?
- Am I responsible for instantiating multiple concurrent invocations of this function?
- It looks like all instances of the function are going to be operating directly on the instance of Pi whose address I pass in; am I responsible for synchronizing access to that memory, or does the Pi type handle this for me?

One function raises all these questions. Imagine a program of any moderate size, and you can begin to understand the complexities concurrency can pose.

Comments can work wonders here. What if the `CalculatePi` function were instead written like this:

```
// CalculatePi calculates digits of Pi between the begin and end
// place.
//
// Internally, CalculatePi will create FLOOR((end-begin)/2) concurrent
// processes which recursively call CalculatePi. Synchronization of
// writes to pi are handled internally by the Pi struct.
func CalculatePi(begin, end int64, pi *Pi)
```

We now understand that we can call the function plainly and not worry about concurrency or synchronization. Importantly, the comment covers these aspects:

- Who is responsible for the concurrency?
- How is the problem space mapped onto concurrency primitives?
- Who is responsible for the synchronization?

When exposing functions, methods, and variables in problem spaces that involve concurrency, do your colleagues and future self a favor: err on the side of verbose comments, and try and cover these three aspects.

Also consider that perhaps the ambiguity in this function suggests that we've modeled it wrong. Maybe we should instead take a functional approach and ensure our function has no side effects:

```
func CalculatePi(begin, end int64) []uint
```

The signature of this function alone removes any questions of synchronization, but still leaves the question of whether concurrency is used. We can modify the signature again to throw out another signal as to what is happening:

```
func CalculatePi(begin, end int64) <-chan uint
```

Here we see the first usage of what's called a *channel*. For reasons we'll explore later in the section "Channels" on page 64, this suggests that `CalculatePi` will at least have one goroutine and that we shouldn't bother with creating our own.

These modifications then have performance ramifications that have to be taken into consideration, and we're back to the problem of balancing clarity with performance. Clarity is important because we want to make it as likely as possible that people working with this code in the future will do the right thing, and performance is important for obvious reasons. The two aren't mutually exclusive, but they are difficult to mix.

Now consider these difficulties in communication and try and scale them up to team-sized projects.

Wow, this is a problem.

The good news is that Go has made progress in making these types of problems easier to solve. The language itself favors readability and simplicity. The way it encourages modeling your concurrent code encourages correctness, composability, and scalability. In fact, the way Go handles concurrency can actually help express problem domains more clearly! Let's take a look at why this is the case.

Simplicity in the Face of Complexity

So far, I've painted a pretty grim picture. Concurrency is certainly a difficult area in computer science, but I want to leave you with hope: these problems aren't intractable, and with Go's concurrency primitives, you can more safely and clearly express your concurrent algorithms. The runtime and communication difficulties we've discussed are by no means solved by Go, but they have been made significantly easier. In the next chapter, we'll discover the root of how this progress has been accomplished. Here, let's spend a little time exploring the idea that Go's concurrency primitives can actually make it easier to model problem domains and express algorithms more clearly.

Go's runtime does most of the heavy lifting and provides the foundation for most of Go's concurrency niceties. We'll save the discussion of how it all works for Chapter 6, but here we'll discuss how these things make your life easier.

Let's first discuss Go's concurrent, low-latency, garbage collector. There is often debate among developers as to whether garbage collectors are a good thing to have in a language. Detractors suggest that garbage collectors prevent work in any problem domain that requires real-time performance or a deterministic performance profile—that pausing all activity in a program to clean up garbage simply isn't acceptable. While there is some merit to this, the excellent work that has been done on Go's garbage collector has dramatically reduced the audience that needs to concern themselves with the minutia of how Go's garbage collection works. As of Go 1.8, garbage collection pauses are generally between 10 and 100 microseconds!

How does this help you? Memory management can be another difficult problem domain in computer science, and when combined with concurrency, it can become extraordinarily difficult to write correct code. If you're in the majority of developers who don't need to worry about pauses as small as 10 microseconds, Go has made it much easier to use concurrency in your program by not forcing you to manage memory, let alone across concurrent processes.

Go's runtime also automatically handles multiplexing concurrent operations onto operating system threads. That's a mouthful, and we'll see exactly what that means in the section on "Goroutines" on page 37. For the purposes of understanding how this helps you, all you need to know is that it allows you to directly map concurrent problems into concurrent constructs instead of dealing with the minutia of starting and managing threads, and mapping logic evenly across available threads.

For example, say you write a web server, and you'd like every connection accepted to be handled concurrently with every other connection. In some languages, before your web server begins accepting connections, you'd likely have to create a collection of threads, commonly called a *thread pool*, and then map incoming connections onto threads. Then, within each thread you've created, you'd need to loop over all the connections on that thread to ensure they were all receiving some CPU time. In addition, you'd have to write your connection-handling logic to be pausable so that it shares fairly with the other connections.

Whew! In contrast, in Go you would write a function and then prepend its invocation with the go keyword. The runtime handles everything else we discussed automatically! When you're going through the process of designing your program, under which model do you think you're more likely to reach for concurrency? Which do you think is more likely to turn out correct?

Go's concurrency primitives also make composing larger problems easier. As we'll see in the section "Channels" on page 64, Go's *channel* primitive provides a composable, concurrent-safe way to communicate between concurrent processes.

I've glossed over most of the details of how these things work, but I wanted to give you some sense of how Go invites you to use concurrency in your program to help you solve your problems in a clear and performant way. In the next chapter we'll discuss the philosophy concurrency and why Go got so much right. If you're eager to jump into some code, you might want to flip over to Chapter 3.

CHAPTER 2

Modeling Your Code: Communicating Sequential Processes

The Difference Between Concurrency and Parallelism

The fact that *concurrency* is different from *parallelism* is often overlooked or misunderstood. In conversations between many developers, the two terms are often used interchangeably to mean "something that runs at the same time as something else." Sometimes using the word "parallel" in this context is correct, but usually if the developers are discussing code, they really ought to be using the word "concurrent."

The reason to differentiate goes well beyond pedantry. The difference between concurrency and parallelism turns out to be a very powerful abstraction when modeling your code, and Go takes full advantage of this. Let's take a look at how the two concepts are different so that we can understand the power of this abstraction. We'll start with a very simple statement:

> Concurrency is a property of the code; parallelism is a property of the running program.

That's kind of an interesting distinction. Don't we usually think about these two things the same way? We write our code so that it will execute in parallel. Right?

Well, let's think about that for second. If I write my code with the intent that two chunks of the program will run in parallel, do I have any guarantee that will actually happen when the program is run? What happens if I run the code on a machine with only one core? Some of you may be thinking, *It will run in parallel*, but this isn't true!

The chunks of our program may *appear* to be running in parallel, but really they're executing in a sequential manner faster than is distinguishable. The CPU context switches to share time between different programs, and over a coarse enough granularity of time, the tasks appear to be running in parallel. If we were to run the same binary on a machine with two cores, the program's chunks might actually be running in parallel.

This reveals a few interesting and important things. The first is that we do not write parallel code, only concurrent code that we *hope* will be run in parallel. Once again, parallelism is a property of the *runtime* of our program, not the code.

The second interesting thing is that we see it is possible—maybe even desirable—to be ignorant of whether our concurrent code is actually running in parallel. This is only made possible by the layers of abstraction that lie beneath our program's model: the concurrency primitives, the program's runtime, the operating system, the platform the operating system runs on (in the case of hypervisors, containers, and virtual machines), and ultimately the CPUs. These abstractions are what allow us to make the distinction between concurrency and parallelism, and ultimately what give us the power and flexibility to express ourselves. We'll come back to this.

The third and final interesting thing is that parallelism is a function of time, or context. Remember in "Atomicity" on page 6 where we discussed the concept of context? There, context was defined as the bounds by which an operation was considered atomic. Here, it's defined as the bounds by which two or more operations could be considered parallel.

For example, if our context was a space of five seconds, and we ran two operations that each took a second to run, we would consider the operations to have run in parallel. If our context was one second, we would consider the operations to have run sequentially.

It may not do us much good to go about redefining our context in terms of time slices, but remember context isn't constrained to time. We can define a context as the process our program runs within, its operating system thread, or its machine. This is important because the context you define is closely related to the concept of concurrency and correctness. Just as atomic operations can be considered atomic depending on the context you define, concurrent operations are correct depending on the context you define. It's all relative.

That's a bit abstract, so let's look at an example. Let's say the context we're discussing is your computer. Theoretical physics aside, we can reasonably expect that a process executing on my machine isn't going to affect the logic of a process on your machine. If we both start a calculator process and begin performing some simple arithmetic, the calculations I perform shouldn't affect the calculations you perform.

It's a silly example, but if we break it down, we see all the pieces in play: our machines are the context, and the processes are the concurrent operations. In this case, we have chosen to model our concurrent operations by thinking of the world in terms of separate computers, operating systems, and processes. These abstractions allow us to confidently assert correctness.

Is This Really a Silly Example?

Using individual computers seems like a contrived example to make a point, but personal computers weren't always so ubiquitous! Up until the late 1970s, mainframes were the norm, and the common context developers used when thinking about problems concurrently was a program's process.

Now that many developers are working with distributed systems, it's shifting back the other way! We're now beginning to think in terms of hypervisors, containers, and virtual machines as our concurrent contexts.

We can reasonably expect one process on a machine to remain unaffected by a process on another machine (assuming they're not part of the same distributed system), but can we expect two processes on the *same* machine to not affect the logic of one another? Process A may overwrite some files process B is reading, or in an insecure OS, process A may even corrupt memory process B is reading. Doing so intentionally is how many exploits work.

Still, at the process level, things remain relatively easy to think about. If we return to our calculator example, it's still reasonable to expect that two users running two calculator processes on the same machine should reasonably expect their operations to be logically isolated from one another. Fortunately, the process boundary and the OS help us think about these problems in a logical manner. But we can see that the developer begins to be burdened with some concerns of concurrency, and this problem only gets worse.

What if we move down one more level to the OS thread boundary? It is here that all the problems enumerated in the section "Why Is Concurrency Hard?" on page 4 really come to bear: race conditions, deadlocks, livelocks, and starvation. If we had *one* calculator process that all users on a machine had views into, it would be more difficult to get the concurrent logic right. We would have to begin worrying about synchronizing access to the memory and retrieving the correct results for the correct user.

What's happening is that as we begin moving down the stack of abstraction, the problem of modeling things concurrently is becoming both more difficult to reason about, and more important. Conversely, our abstractions are becoming more and more important to us. In other words, the more difficult it is to get concurrency right, the more important it is to have access to concurrency primitives that are easy to compose. Unfortunately, most concurrent logic in our industry is written at one of the highest levels of abstraction: OS threads.

Before Go was first revealed to the public, this was where the chain of abstraction ended for most of the popular programming languages. If you wanted to write concurrent code, you would model your program in terms of threads and synchronize the access to the memory between them. If you had a lot of things you had to model concurrently and your machine couldn't handle that many threads, you created a *thread pool* and multiplexed your operations onto the thread pool.

Go has added another link in that chain: the *goroutine*. In addition, Go has borrowed several concepts from the work of famed computer scientist Tony Hoare, and introduced new primitives for us to use, namely *channels*.

If we continue the line of reasoning we have been following, we'd assume that introducing another level of abstraction below OS threads would bring with it more difficulties, but the interesting thing is that it *doesn't*. It actually makes things *easier*. This is because we haven't really added another layer of abstraction on top of OS threads, we've supplanted them.

Threads are still there, of course, but we find that we rarely have to think about our problem space in terms of OS threads. Instead, we model things in goroutines and channels, and occasionally shared memory. This leads to some interesting properties that we explore in the section "How This Helps You" on page 29. But first, let's take a closer look at where Go got a lot of its ideas—the paper at the root of Go's concurrency primitives: Tony Hoare's seminal paper, "Communicating Sequential Processes."

What Is CSP?

When Go is discussed, you'll often hear people throw around the acronym *CSP*. Often in the same breath it's lauded as the reason for Go's success, or a panacea for concurrent programming. It's enough to make people who don't know what CSP is begin to think that computer science had discovered some new technique that magically makes programming concurrent programs as simple as writing procedural ones. While CSP does make things easier, and programs more robust, it is unfortunately not a miracle. So what is it? What has everyone so excited?

CSP stands for "Communicating Sequential Processes," which is both a technique and the name of the paper that introduced it. In 1978, Charles Antony Richard Hoare published the paper (*http://bit.ly/HoareCSP*) in the Association for Computing Machinery (more popularly referred to as ACM).

In this paper, Hoare suggests that input and output are two overlooked primitives of programming—particularly in concurrent code. At the time Hoare authored this paper, research was still being done on how to structure programs, but most of this effort was being directed to techniques for sequential code: usage of the goto statement was being debated, and the object-oriented paradigm was beginning to take root. Concurrent operations weren't being given much thought. Hoare set out to correct this, and thus his paper, and CSP, were born.

In the 1978 paper, CSP was only a simple programming language constructed solely to demonstrate the power of communicating sequential processes; in fact, he even says in the paper:

> Thus the concepts and notations introduced in this paper should … not be regarded as suitable for use as a programming language, either for abstract or for concrete programming.

Hoare was deeply concerned that the techniques he was presenting did nothing to further the study of correctness of programs, and that the techniques may not be performant in a real language based on his own. Over the next six years, the idea of CSP was refined into a formal representation of something called *process calculus* in an effort to take the ideas of communicating sequential processes and actually begin to reason about program correctness. Process calculus is a way to mathematically model concurrent systems and also provides algebraic laws to perform transformations on these systems to analyze their various properties, e.g., efficiency and correctness. Although process calculi are an interesting topic in their own right, they are beyond the scope of this book. And since the original paper on CSP and the language that evolved from it were largely the inspiration for Go's concurrency model, it's these we'll focus on.

To support his assertion that inputs and outputs needed to be considered language primitives, Hoare's CSP programming language contained primitives to model input and output, or *communication*, between *processes* correctly (this is where the paper's name comes from). Hoare applied the term *processes* to any encapsulated portion of logic that required input to run and produced output other processes would consume. Hoare probably could have used the word "function" were it not for the debate on how to structure programs occurring in the community when he wrote his paper.

For communication between the processes, Hoare created input and output *commands*: ! for sending input into a process, and ? for reading output from a process. Each command had to specify either an output variable (in the case of reading a variable out of a process), or a destination (in the case of sending input to a process). Sometimes these two would refer to the same thing, in which case the two processes would be said to *correspond*. In other words, output from one process would flow directly into the input of another process. Table 2-1 shows a few examples from the paper.

Table 2-1. An extract of some examples from Hoare's CSP paper

Operation	Explanation
cardreader?card image	From cardreader, read a card and assign its value (an array of characters) to the variable cardimage.
lineprinter!line image	To lineprinter, send the value of lineimage for printing.
X?(x, y)	From process named X, input a pair of values and assign them to x and y.
DIV!(3*a+b, 13)	To process DIV, output the two specified values.
*[c:character; west?c → east!c]	Read all the characters output by west, and output them one by one to east. The repetition terminates when the process west terminates.

The similarities to Go's channels are apparent. Notice how in the last example the output from west was sent to a variable c and the input to east was received from the same variable. These two processes correspond. In Hoare's first paper on CSP, processes could only communicate via named sources and destinations. He acknowledged that this would cause issues with embedding code as a library, as consumers of the code would have to know the names of the inputs and outputs. He casually mentioned the possibility of registering what he called "port names," in which names could be declared in the head of the parallel command, something we would probably recognize as named parameters and named return values.

The language also utilized a so-called *guarded command*, which Edgar Dijkstra had introduced in a previous paper written in 1974, "Guarded commands, nondeterminacy and formal derivation of programs" (*http://bit.ly/DijkstraGuarded*). A guarded command is simply a statement with a left- and righthand side, split by a →. The lefthand side served as a conditional, or *guard* for the righthand side in that if the lefthand side was false or, in the case of a command, returned false or had exited, the righthand side would never be executed. Combining these with Hoare's I/O commands laid the foundation for Hoare's communicating processes, and thus Go's channels.

Using these primitives, Hoare walked through several examples and demonstrated how a language with first-class support for modeling communication makes solving problems simpler and easier to comprehend. Some of the notation he uses is a little terse (perl programmers would probably disagree!), but the problems he presents have extraordinarily clear solutions. Similar solutions in Go are a bit longer, but also carry with them this clarity.

History has judged Hoare's suggestion to be correct; however, it's interesting to note that before Go was released, few languages have really brought support for these primitives into the language. Most popular languages favor sharing and synchronizing access to the memory to CSP's message-passing style. There are exceptions, but unfortunately these are confined to languages that haven't seen wide adoption. Go is one of the first languages to incorporate principles from CSP in its core, and bring this style of concurrent programming to the masses. Its success has led other languages to attempt to add these primitives as well.

Memory access synchronization isn't inherently bad. We'll see later in the chapter (in "Go's Philosophy on Concurrency" on page 31) that sometimes sharing memory is appropriate in certain situations, even in Go. However, the shared memory model *can* be difficult to utilize correctly—especially in large or complicated programs. It's for this reason that concurrency is considered one of Go's strengths: it has been built from the start with principles from CSP in mind and therefore it is easy to read, write, and reason about.

How This Helps You

You may or may not find all of this fascinating, but chances are that if you're reading this book you have problems to solve, and you're wondering why any of this matters. What does Go do so differently that has set it apart from other popular languages when it comes to concurrency?

As we discussed in the section "The Difference Between Concurrency and Parallelism" on page 23 for modeling concurrent problems, it's common for languages to end their chain of abstraction at the level of the OS thread and memory access synchronization. Go takes a different route and supplants this with the concept of goroutines and channels.

If we were to draw a comparison between concepts in the two ways of abstracting concurrent code, we'd probably compare the goroutine to a thread, and a channel to a mutex (these primitives only have a passing resemblance, but hopefully the comparison helps you get your bearings). What do these different abstractions do for us?

Goroutines free us from having to think about our problem space in terms of parallelism and instead allow us to model problems closer to their natural level of concurrency. Although we went over the difference between concurrency and parallelism, how that difference affects how we model solutions might not be clear. Let's jump into an example.

Let's say I need to build a web server that fields requests on an endpoint. Setting aside frameworks for a moment, in a language that only offers a thread abstraction, I would probably be ruminating on the following questions:

- Does my language naturally support threads, or will I have to pick a library?
- Where should my thread confinement boundaries be?
- How heavy are threads in this operating system?

- How do the operating systems my program will be running in handle threads differently?

- I should create a pool of workers to constrain the number of threads I create. How do I find the optimal number?

All of these are important things to consider, but none of them directly concern the problem you're trying to solve. You've immediately been yanked down into the technicalities of how you're going to solve the problem of parallelism.

If we step back and think about the natural problem, we could state it as such: individual users are connecting to my endpoint and opening a session. The session should field their request and return a response. In Go, we can almost directly represent the natural state of this problem in code: we would create a goroutine for each incoming connection, field the request there (potentially communicating with other goroutines for data/services), and then return from the goroutine's function. How we naturally think about the problem maps directly to the natural way to code things in Go.

This is achieved by a promise Go makes to us: that goroutines are lightweight, and we normally won't have to worry about creating one. There are appropriate times to consider how many goroutines are running in your system, but doing so upfront is soundly a premature optimization. Contrast this with threads where you would be wise to consider such matters upfront.

Just because there is a framework available for a language that abstracts the concerns of parallelism away for you, doesn't mean this natural way of modeling concurrent problems doesn't matter! Someone has to write the framework, and your code will be sitting on top of whatever complexity the author(s) had to deal with. Just because the complexity is hidden from you doesn't mean it's not there, and complexity breeds bugs. In the case of Go, the language was designed around concurrency, so the language is not incongruent with the concurrency primitives it provides. This means less friction and fewer bugs!

A more natural mapping to the problem space is an *enormous* benefit, but it has a few beneficial side effects as well. Go's runtime multiplexes goroutines onto OS threads automatically and manages their scheduling for us. This means that optimizations to the runtime can be made without us having to change how we've modeled our problem; this is classic separation of concerns. As advancements in parallelism are made, Go's runtime will improve, as will the performance of your program—all for free. Keep an eye on Go's release notes and occasionally you'll see things like:

```
In Go 1.5, the order in which goroutines are scheduled has been changed.
```

The Go authors are making improvements behind the scenes to make your program faster.

This decoupling of concurrency and parallelism has another benefit: because Go's runtime is managing the scheduling of goroutines for you, it can introspect on things like goroutines blocked waiting for I/O and intelligently reallocate OS threads to goroutines that are not blocked. This also increases the performance of your code. We'll discuss more of what Go's runtime does for you in Chapter 6.

Yet another benefit of the more natural mapping between problem spaces and Go code is the likely increased amount of the problem space modeled in a concurrent manner. Because the problems we work on as developers are naturally concurrent more often than not, we'll naturally be writing concurrent code at a finer level of granularity than we perhaps would in other languages; e.g., if we go back to our web server example, we would now have a goroutine for every user instead of connections multiplexed onto a thread pool. This finer level of granularity enables our program to scale *dynamically* when it runs to the amount of parallelism possible on the program's host—Amdahl's law in action! That's kind of amazing.

And goroutines are only one piece of the puzzle. The other concepts from CSP, channels and select statements, add value as well.

Channels, for instance, are inherently *composable* with other channels. This makes writing large systems simpler because you can coordinate the input from multiple subsystems by easily composing the output together. You can combine input channels with timeouts, cancellations, or messages to other subsystems. Coordinating mutexes is a much more difficult proposition.

The `select` statement is the complement to Go's channels and is what enables all the difficult bits of composing channels. `select` statements allow you to efficiently wait for events, select a message from competing channels in a uniform random way, continue on if there are no messages waiting, and more.

This wonderful tapestry of primitives inspired by CSP and the runtime that supports it are the things that power Go. We'll spend the rest of the book discovering how these things work, why, and how we can use them to write amazing code.

Go's Philosophy on Concurrency

CSP was and *is* a large part of what Go was designed around; however, Go also supports more traditional means of writing concurrent code through memory access synchronization and the primitives that follow that technique. Structs and methods in the `sync` and other packages allow you to perform locks, create pools of resources, preempt goroutines, and more.

This ability to choose between CSP primitives and memory access synchronizations is great for you since it gives you a little more control over what style of concurrent code you choose to write to solve problems, but it can also be a little confusing. Newcomers to the language often get the impression that the CSP style of concurrency is considered the one and only way to write concurrent code in Go. For instance, in the documentation for the sync package, it says:

> Package sync provides basic synchronization primitives such as mutual exclusion locks. Other than the Once and WaitGroup types, most are intended for use by low-level library routines. Higher-level synchronization is better done via channels and communication.

In the language FAQ (*https://golang.org/doc/faq*), it says:

> Regarding mutexes, the sync package implements them, but we hope Go programming style will encourage people to try higher-level techniques. In particular, consider structuring your program so that only one goroutine at a time is ever responsible for a particular piece of data.

> Do not communicate by sharing memory. Instead, share memory by communicating.

There are also numerous articles, lectures, and interviews where various members of the Go core team espouse the CSP style over primitives like sync.Mutex.

It is therefore completely understandable to be confused as to why the Go team chose to expose memory access synchronization primitives at all. What may be even more confusing is that you'll see synchronization primitives commonly out in the wild, see people complain about overuse of channels, and also hear some of the Go team members stating that it's OK to use them. Here's a quote from the Go Wiki (*https:// github.com/golang/go/wiki/MutexOrChannel*) on the matter:

> One of Go's mottos is "Share memory by communicating, don't communicate by sharing memory."

> That said, Go does provide traditional locking mechanisms in the sync package. Most locking issues can be solved using either channels or traditional locks.

> So which should you use?

> Use whichever is most expressive and/or most simple.

That's good advice, and this is a guideline you often see when working with Go, but it is a little vague. How do we understand what is more expressive and/or simpler? What criteria can we use? Fortunately there are some guideposts we can use to help us do the correct thing. As we'll see, the way we can mostly differentiate comes from where we're trying to manage our concurrency: internally to a tight scope, or externally throughout our system. Figure 2-1 enumerates these guideposts into a decision tree.

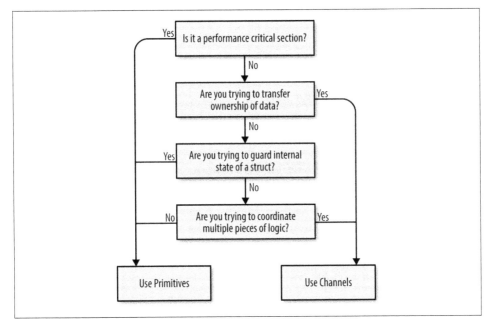

Figure 2-1. Decision tree

Let's step through these decision points one by one:

Are you trying to transfer ownership of data?
> If you have a bit of code that produces a result and wants to share that result with another bit of code, what you're really doing is transferring ownership of that data. If you're familiar with the concept of memory-ownership in languages that don't support garbage collection, this is the same idea: data has an owner, and one way to make concurrent programs safe is to ensure only one concurrent context has ownership of data at a time. Channels help us communicate this concept by encoding that intent into the channel's type.

> One large benefit of doing so is you can create buffered channels to implement a cheap in-memory queue and thus decouple your producer from your consumer. Another is that by using channels, you've implicitly made your concurrent code *composable* with other concurrent code.

Are you trying to guard internal state of a struct?
> This is a great candidate for memory access synchronization primitives, and a pretty strong indicator that you shouldn't use channels. By using memory access synchronization primitives, you can hide the implementation detail of locking your critical section from your callers. Here's a small example of a type that is thread-safe, but doesn't expose that complexity to its callers:

```
type Counter struct {
    mu sync.Mutex
    value int
}
func (c *Counter) Increment() {
    c.mu.Lock()
    defer c.mu.Unlock()
    c.value++
}
```

If you recall the concept of atomicity, we can say that what we've done here is defined the scope of atomicity for the Counter type. Calls to Increment can be considered atomic.

Remember the key word here is *internal*. If you find yourself exposing locks beyond a type, this should raise a red flag. Try to keep the locks constrained to a small lexical scope.

Are you trying to coordinate multiple pieces of logic?
Remember that channels are inherently more composable than memory access synchronization primitives. Having locks scattered throughout your object-graph sounds like a nightmare, but having channels everywhere is expected and encouraged! I can compose channels, but I can't easily compose locks or methods that return values.

You will find it much easier to control the emergent complexity that arises in your software if you use channels because of Go's select statement, and their ability to serve as queues and be safely passed around. If you find yourself struggling to understand how your concurrent code works, why a deadlock or race is occurring, and you're using primitives, this is probably a good indicator that you should switch to channels.

Is it a performance-critical section?
This absolutely does *not* mean, "I want my program to be performant, therefore I will only use mutexes." Rather, if you have a section of your program that you have profiled, and it turns out to be a major bottleneck that is orders of magnitude slower than the rest of the program, using memory access synchronization primitives may help this critical section perform under load. This is because channels *use* memory access synchronization to operate, therefore they can only be slower. Before we even consider this, however, a performance-critical section might be hinting that we need to restructure our program.

Hopefully, this gives some clarity around whether to utilize CSP-style concurrency or memory access synchronization. There are other patterns and practices that are useful in languages that use the OS thread as the means of abstracting concurrency. For example, things like thread pools often come up. Because most of these abstractions are targeted toward the strengths and weaknesses of OS threads, a good rule of thumb when working with Go is to discard these patterns. That's not to say they aren't useful at all, but the use cases are certainly much more constrained in Go. Stick to modeling your problem space with goroutines, use them to represent the concurrent parts of your workflow, and don't be afraid to be liberal when starting them. You're much more likely to need to restructure your program than you are to begin running into the upper limit of how many goroutines your hardware can support.

Go's philosophy on concurrency can be summed up like this: aim for simplicity, use channels when possible, and treat goroutines like a free resource.

CHAPTER 3

Go's Concurrency Building Blocks

In this chapter, we'll discuss Go's rich tapestry of features that support its concurrency story. By the end of this chapter, you should have a good understanding of the syntax, functions, and packages available to you, and their functionality.

Goroutines

Goroutines are one of the most basic units of organization in a Go program, so it's important we understand what they are and how they work. In fact, every Go program has at least one goroutine: the *main goroutine*, which is automatically created and started when the process begins. In almost any program you'll probably find yourself reaching for a goroutine sooner or later to assist in solving your problems. So what are they?

Put very simply, a goroutine is a function that is running concurrently (remember: not necessarily in parallel!) alongside other code. You can start one simply by placing the go keyword before a function:

```
func main() {
    go sayHello()
    // continue doing other things
}

func sayHello() {
    fmt.Println("hello")
}
```

Anonymous functions work too! Here's an example that does the same thing as the previous example; however, instead of creating a goroutine from a function, we create a goroutine from an anonymous function:

```
go func() {
    fmt.Println("hello")
}() ❶
// continue doing other things
```

❶ Notice that we must invoke the anonymous function immediately to use the go keyword.

Alternatively, you can assign the function to a variable and call the anonymous function like this:

```
sayHello := func() {
    fmt.Println("hello")
}
go sayHello()
// continue doing other things
```

How cool is this! We can create a concurrent block of logic with a function and a single keyword! Believe it or not, that's all you need to know to start goroutines. There's a lot to be said regarding how to use them properly, synchronize them, and organize them, but this is really all you need to know to begin utilizing them. The rest of this chapter goes deeper into what goroutines *are* and how they work. If you're only interested in writing some code that works properly with goroutines, you may consider skipping ahead to the next section.

So let's look at what's happening behind the scenes here: how do goroutines actually work? Are they OS threads? Green threads? How many can we create?

Goroutines are unique to Go (though some other languages have a concurrency primitive that is similar). They're not OS threads, and they're not exactly green threads—threads that are managed by a language's runtime—they're a higher level of abstraction known as *coroutines*. Coroutines are simply concurrent subroutines (functions, closures, or methods in Go) that are *nonpreemptive*—that is, they cannot be interrupted. Instead, coroutines have multiple points throughout which allow for suspension or reentry.

What makes goroutines unique to Go are their deep integration with Go's runtime. Goroutines don't define their own suspension or reentry points; Go's runtime observes the runtime behavior of goroutines and automatically suspends them when they block and then resumes them when they become unblocked. In a way this makes them preemptable, but only at points where the goroutine has become blocked. It is an elegant partnership between the runtime and a goroutine's logic. Thus, goroutines can be considered a special class of coroutine.

Coroutines, and thus goroutines, are implicitly concurrent constructs, but concurrency is not a property *of* a coroutine: something must host several coroutines simultaneously and give each an opportunity to execute—otherwise, they wouldn't be concurrent! Note that this does not imply that coroutines are implicitly parallel. It is certainly possible to have several coroutines executing sequentially to give the illusion of parallelism, and in fact this happens all the time in Go.

Go's mechanism for hosting goroutines is an implementation of what's called an *M:N scheduler*, which means it maps M green threads to N OS threads. Goroutines are then scheduled onto the green threads. When we have more goroutines than green threads available, the scheduler handles the distribution of the goroutines across the available threads and ensures that when these goroutines become blocked, other goroutines can be run. We'll discuss how all of this works in Chapter 6, but here we'll cover how Go models concurrency.

Go follows a model of concurrency called the *fork-join* model.[1] The word *fork* refers to the fact that at any point in the program, it can split off a *child* branch of execution to be run concurrently with its *parent*. The word *join* refers to the fact that at some point in the future, these concurrent branches of execution will join back together. Where the child rejoins the parent is called a *join point*. Here's a graphical representation to help you picture it:

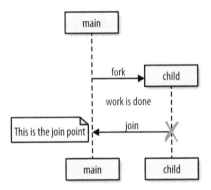

The go statement is how Go performs a fork, and the forked threads of execution are goroutines. Let's return to our simple goroutine example:

```
sayHello := func() {
    fmt.Println("hello")
}
go sayHello()
// continue doing other things
```

---

1 Those of you familiar with C may be considering drawing a comparison between this model and the fork function. The fork-join model is a *logical* model of how concurrency is performed. It does describe a C program that calls fork and then wait, but only at a logical level. The fork-join model says nothing about how memory is managed.

Here, the sayHello function will be run on its own goroutine, while the rest of the program continues executing. In this example, there is no join point. The goroutine executing sayHello will simply exit at some undetermined time in the future, and the rest of the program will have already continued executing.

However, there is one problem with this example: as written, it's undetermined whether the sayHello function will ever be run at all. The goroutine will be *created* and scheduled with Go's runtime to execute, but it may not actually get a chance to run before the main goroutine exits.

Indeed, because we omit the rest of the rest of the main function for simplicity, when we run this small example, it is almost certain that the program will finish executing before the goroutine hosting the call to sayHello is ever started. As a result, you won't see the word "hello" printed to stdout. You could put a time.Sleep after you create the goroutine, but recall that this doesn't actually create a join point, only a race condition. If you recall Chapter 1, you increase the probability that the goroutine will run before exiting, but you do not guarantee it. Join points are what guarantee our program's correctness and remove the race condition.

In order to a create a join point, you have to synchronize the main goroutine and the sayHello goroutine. This can be done in a number of ways, but I'll use one we'll talk about in "The sync Package" on page 47: sync.WaitGroup. Right now it's not important to understand how this example creates a join point, only that it creates one between the two goroutines. Here's a correct version of our example:

```
var wg sync.WaitGroup
sayHello := func() {
    defer wg.Done()
    fmt.Println("hello")
}
wg.Add(1)
go sayHello()
wg.Wait() ❶
```

❶ This is the join point.

This produces:

```
hello
```

This example will deterministically block the main goroutine until the goroutine hosting the sayHello function terminates. You'll learn how sync.WaitGroup works in "The sync Package" on page 47, but to make our examples correct, I'll begin using it to create join points.

We've been using a lot of anonymous functions in our examples to create quick goroutine examples. Let's shift our attention to closures. Closures close around the lexical scope they are created in, thereby capturing variables. If you run a closure in a goroutine, does the closure operate on a copy of these variables, or the original references? Let's give it a try and see:

```
var wg sync.WaitGroup
salutation := "hello"
wg.Add(1)
go func() {
    defer wg.Done()
    salutation = "welcome" ❶
}()
wg.Wait()
fmt.Println(salutation)
```

❶ Here we see the goroutine modifying the value of the variable salutation.

What do you think the value of salutation will be: "hello" or "welcome"? Let's run it and find out:

```
welcome
```

Interesting! It turns out that goroutines execute within the same address space they were created in, and so our program prints out the word "welcome." Let's try another example. What do you think this program will output?

```
var wg sync.WaitGroup
for _, salutation := range []string{"hello", "greetings", "good day"} {
    wg.Add(1)
    go func() {
        defer wg.Done()
        fmt.Println(salutation) ❶
    }()
}
wg.Wait()
```

❶ Here we reference the loop variable salutation created by ranging over a string slice.

The answer is trickier than most people expect, and is one of the few surprising things in Go. Most people intuitively think this will print out the words "hello," "greetings," and "good day" in some nondeterministic order, but look what it does:

```
good day
good day
good day
```

That's kind of surprising! Let's figure out what's going on here. In this example, the goroutine is running a closure that has closed over the iteration variable salutation, which has a type of string. As our loop iterates, salutation is being assigned to the next string value in the slice literal. Because the goroutines being scheduled may run at any point in time in the future, it is undetermined what values will be printed from within the goroutine. On my machine, there is a high probability the loop will exit before the goroutines are begun. This means the `salutation` variable falls out of scope. What happens then? Can the goroutines still reference something that has fallen out of scope? Won't the goroutines be accessing memory that has potentially been garbage collected?

This is an interesting side note about how Go manages memory. The Go runtime is observant enough to know that a reference to the `salutation` variable is still being held, and therefore will transfer the memory to the heap so that the goroutines can continue to access it.

Usually on my machine, the loop exits before any goroutines begin running, so `salutation` is transferred to the heap holding a reference to the last value in my string slice, "good day." And so I usually see "good day" printed three times. The proper way to write this loop is to pass a copy of `salutation` into the closure so that by the time the goroutine is run, it will be operating on the data from its iteration of the loop:

```
var wg sync.WaitGroup
for _, salutation := range []string{"hello", "greetings", "good day"} {
    wg.Add(1)
    go func(salutation string) { ❶
        defer wg.Done()
        fmt.Println(salutation)
    }(salutation) ❷
}
wg.Wait()
```

❶ Here we declare a parameter, just like any other function. We shadow the original `salutation` variable to make what's happening more apparent.

❷ Here we pass in the current iteration's variable to the closure. A copy of the string struct is made, thereby ensuring that when the goroutine is run, we refer to the proper string.

And as we see, we get the correct output:

```
good day
hello
greetings
```

This example behaves as we would expect it to, and is only slightly more verbose.

Because goroutines operate within the same address space as each other, and simply host functions, utilizing goroutines is a natural extension to writing nonconcurrent code. Go's compiler nicely takes care of pinning variables in memory so that goroutines don't accidentally access freed memory, which allows developers to focus on their problem space instead of memory management; however, it's not a blank check.

Since multiple goroutines can operate against the same address space, we still have to worry about synchronization. As we've discussed, we can choose either to synchronize access to the shared memory the goroutines access, or we can use CSP primitives to share memory by communication. We'll discuss these techniques later in the chapter in "Channels" on page 64 and "The sync Package" on page 47.

Yet another benefit of goroutines is that they're extraordinarily lightweight. Here's an excerpt from the Go FAQ (*https://golang.org/doc/faq#goroutines*):

> A newly minted goroutine is given a few kilobytes, which is almost always enough. When it isn't, the run-time grows (and shrinks) the memory for storing the stack automatically, allowing many goroutines to live in a modest amount of memory. The CPU overhead averages about three cheap instructions per function call. It is practical to create hundreds of thousands of goroutines in the same address space. If goroutines were just threads, system resources would run out at a much smaller number.

A few kilobytes per goroutine; that isn't bad at all! Let's try and verify that for ourselves. But before we do, we have to cover one interesting thing about goroutines: the garbage collector does nothing to collect goroutines that have been abandoned somehow. If I write the following:

```
go func() {
    // <operation that will block forever>
}()
// Do work
```

The goroutine here will hang around until the process exits. We'll discuss how to address this in Chapter 4 in the section "Preventing Goroutine Leaks" on page 90. We'll use this to our advantage in the next example to actually measure the size of a goroutine.

In the following example, we combine the fact that goroutines are not garbage collected with the runtime's ability to introspect upon itself and measure the amount of memory allocated before and after goroutine creation:

```
memConsumed := func() uint64 {
    runtime.GC()
    var s runtime.MemStats
    runtime.ReadMemStats(&s)
    return s.Sys
}

var c <-chan interface{}
var wg sync.WaitGroup
noop := func() { wg.Done(); <-c }  ❶

const numGoroutines = 1e4  ❷
wg.Add(numGoroutines)
before := memConsumed()  ❸
for i := numGoroutines; i > 0; i-- {
    go noop()
```

```
}
wg.Wait()
after := memConsumed()  ❹
fmt.Printf("%.3fkb", float64(after-before)/numGoroutines/1000)
```

❶ We require a goroutine that will never exit so that we can keep a number of them in memory for measurement. Don't worry about how we're achieving this at this time; just know that this goroutine won't exit until the process is finished.

❷ Here we define the number of goroutines to create. We will use the law of large numbers to asymptotically approach the size of a goroutine.

❸ Here we measure the amount of memory consumed before creating our goroutines.

❹ And here we measure the amount of memory consumed after creating our goroutines.

And here's the result:

```
2.817kb
```

It looks like the documentation is correct! These are just empty goroutines that don't do anything, but it still gives us an idea of the number of goroutines we can likely create. Table 3-1 gives some rough estimates of how many goroutines you could likely create with a 64-bit CPU without using swap space.

Table 3-1. Analysis of the rough number of goroutines possible within given memory

Memory (GB)	Goroutines (#/100,000)	Order of magnitude
2^0	3.718	3
2^1	7.436	3
2^2	14.873	6
2^3	29.746	6
2^4	59.492	6
2^5	118.983	6
2^6	237.967	6
2^7	475.934	6
2^8	951.867	6
2^9	1903.735	9

Those numbers are quite large! On my laptop I have 8 GB of RAM, which means that in theory I can spin up *millions* of goroutines without requiring swapping. Of course this ignores other things running on my computer, and the actual contents of the goroutines, but this quick calculation demonstrates just how lightweight goroutines are!

Something that might dampen our spirits is *context switching*, which is when something hosting a concurrent process must save its state to switch to running a different concurrent process. If we have too many concurrent processes, we can spend all of our CPU time context switching between them and never get any real work done. At the OS level, with threads, this can be quite costly. The OS thread must save things like register values, lookup tables, and memory maps to successfully be able to switch back to the current thread when it is time. Then it has to load the same information for the incoming thread.

Context switching in software is comparatively much, much cheaper. Under a software-defined scheduler, the runtime can be more selective in what is persisted for retrieval, how it is persisted, and when the persisting need occur. Let's take a look at the relative performance of context switching on my laptop between OS threads and goroutines. First, we'll utilize Linux's built-in benchmarking suite to measure how long it takes to send a message between two threads on the same core:

```
taskset -c 0 perf bench sched pipe -T
```

This produces:

```
# Running 'sched/pipe' benchmark:
# Executed 1000000 pipe operations between two threads

     Total time: 2.935 [sec]

       2.935784 usecs/op
         340624 ops/sec
```

This benchmark actually measures the time it takes to send *and* receive a message on a thread, so we'll take the result and divide it by two. That gives us 1.467 µs per context switch. That doesn't seem too bad, but let's reserve judgment until we examine context switches between goroutines.

We'll construct a similar benchmark using Go. I've used a few things we haven't discussed yet, so if anything is confusing, just follow the callouts and focus on the result. The following example will create two goroutines and send a message between them:

```
func BenchmarkContextSwitch(b *testing.B) {
    var wg sync.WaitGroup
    begin := make(chan struct{})
    c := make(chan struct{})

    var token struct{}
    sender := func() {
        defer wg.Done()
        <-begin ❶
        for i := 0; i < b.N; i++ {
```

```
            c <- token ❷
        }
    }
    receiver := func() {
        defer wg.Done()
        <-begin ❶
        for i := 0; i < b.N; i++ {
            <-c ❸
        }
    }

    wg.Add(2)
    go sender()
    go receiver()
    b.StartTimer() ❹
    close(begin) ❺
    wg.Wait()
}
```

❶ Here we wait until we're told to begin. We don't want the cost of setting up and starting each goroutine to factor into the measurement of context switching.

❷ Here we send messages to the receiver goroutine. A struct{}{} is called an *empty struct* and takes up no memory; thus, we are only measuring the time it takes to signal a message.

❸ Here we receive a message but do nothing with it.

❹ Here we begin the performance timer.

❺ Here we tell the two goroutines to begin.

We run the benchmark specifying that we only want to utilize one CPU so that it's a similar test to the Linux benchmark. Let's take a look at the results:

```
go test -bench=. -cpu=1 \
src/gos-concurrency-building-blocks/goroutines/fig-ctx-switch_test.go
```

BenchmarkContextSwitch	5000000	225	ns/op
PASS			
ok	command-line-arguments	1.393s	

225 ns per context switch, wow! That's 0.225 µs, or 92% faster than an OS context switch on my machine, which if you recall took 1.467 µs. It's difficult to make any claims about how many goroutines will cause too much context switching, but we can comfortably say that the upper limit is likely not to be any kind of barrier to using goroutines.

Having read this section, you should now understand how to start goroutines and a little about how they work. You should also be confident that you can safely create a goroutine any time you feel the problem space warrants it. As we discussed in the section "The Difference Between Concurrency and Parallelism" on page 23, the more goroutines you create, and if your problem space is not constrained by one concurrent segment per Amdahl's law, the more your program will scale with multiple processors. Creating goroutines is very cheap, and so you should only be discussing their cost if you've proven they are the root cause of a performance issue.

The sync Package

The sync package contains the concurrency primitives that are most useful for low-level memory access synchronization. If you've worked in languages that primarily handle concurrency through memory access synchronization, these types will likely already be familiar to you. The difference between these languages in Go is that Go has built a new set of concurrency primitives on top of the memory access synchronization primitives to provide you with an expanded set of things to work with. As we discussed in "Go's Philosophy on Concurrency" on page 31, these operations have their use—mostly in small scopes such as a struct. It will be up to you to decide when memory access synchronization is appropriate. With that said, let's begin taking a look at the various primitives the sync package exposes.

WaitGroup

WaitGroup is a great way to wait for a set of concurrent operations to complete when you either don't care about the result of the concurrent operation, or you have other means of collecting their results. If neither of those conditions are true, I suggest you use channels and a select statement instead. WaitGroup is so useful, I'm introducing it first so I can use it in subsequent sections. Here's a basic example of using a WaitGroup to wait for goroutines to complete:

```
var wg sync.WaitGroup

wg.Add(1)                        ❶
go func() {
    defer wg.Done()              ❷
    fmt.Println("1st goroutine sleeping...")
    time.Sleep(1)
}()

wg.Add(1)                        ❶
go func() {
    defer wg.Done()              ❷
    fmt.Println("2nd goroutine sleeping...")
    time.Sleep(2)
}()
```

```
    wg.Wait()                              ❸
    fmt.Println("All goroutines complete.")
```

❶ Here we call Add with an argument of 1 to indicate that one goroutine is begin-
    ning.

❷ Here we call Done using the defer keyword to ensure that before we exit the
    goroutine's closure, we indicate to the WaitGroup that we've exited.

❸ Here we call Wait, which will block the main goroutine until all goroutines have
    indicated they have exited.

This produces:

```
2nd goroutine sleeping...
1st goroutine sleeping...
All goroutines complete.
```

You can think of a WaitGroup like a concurrent-safe counter: calls to Add increment
the counter by the integer passed in, and calls to Done decrement the counter by one.
Calls to Wait block until the counter is zero.

Notice that the calls to Add are done outside the goroutines they're helping to track. If
we didn't do this, we would have introduced a race condition, because remember
from "Goroutines" on page 37 that we have no guarantees about when the goroutines
will be scheduled; we could reach the call to Wait before either of the goroutines
begin. Had the calls to Add been placed inside the goroutines' closures, the call to Wait
could have returned without blocking at all because the calls to Add would not have
taken place.

It's customary to couple calls to Add as closely as possible to the goroutines they're
helping to track, but sometimes you'll find Add called to track a group of goroutines
all at once. I usually do this before for loops like this:

```
hello := func(wg *sync.WaitGroup, id int) {
    defer wg.Done()
    fmt.Printf("Hello from %v!\n", id)
}

const numGreeters = 5
var wg sync.WaitGroup
wg.Add(numGreeters)
for i := 0; i < numGreeters; i++ {
    go hello(&wg, i+1)
}
wg.Wait()
```

This produces:

```
Hello from 5!
Hello from 4!
Hello from 3!
Hello from 2!
Hello from 1!
```

Mutex and RWMutex

If you're already familiar with languages that handle concurrency through memory access synchronization, then you'll probably immediately recognize Mutex. If you don't count yourself among that group, don't worry, Mutex is very easy to understand. *Mutex* stands for "mutual exclusion" and is a way to guard critical sections of your program. If you remember from Chapter 1, a critical section is an area of your program that requires exclusive access to a shared resource. A Mutex provides a concurrent-safe way to express exclusive access to these shared resources. To borrow a Goism, whereas channels share memory by communicating, a Mutex shares memory by creating a convention developers must follow to synchronize access to the memory. You are responsible for coordinating access to this memory by guarding access to it with a mutex. Here's a simple example of two goroutines that are attempting to increment and decrement a common value; they use a Mutex to synchronize access:

```
var count int
var lock sync.Mutex

increment := func() {
    lock.Lock()             ❶
    defer lock.Unlock()     ❷
    count++
    fmt.Printf("Incrementing: %d\n", count)
}

decrement := func() {
    lock.Lock()             ❶
    defer lock.Unlock()     ❷
    count--
    fmt.Printf("Decrementing: %d\n", count)
}

// Increment
var arithmetic sync.WaitGroup
for i := 0; i <= 5; i++ {
    arithmetic.Add(1)
    go func() {
        defer arithmetic.Done()
        increment()
    }()
```

```
    }

    // Decrement
    for i := 0; i <= 5; i++ {
        arithmetic.Add(1)
        go func() {
            defer arithmetic.Done()
            decrement()
        }()
    }

    arithmetic.Wait()
    fmt.Println("Arithmetic complete.")
```

❶ Here we request exclusive use of the critical section—in this case the count variable—guarded by a Mutex, lock.

❷ Here we indicate that we're done with the critical section lock is guarding.

This produces:

```
Decrementing: -1
Incrementing: 0
Decrementing: -1
Incrementing: 0
Decrementing: -1
Decrementing: -2
Decrementing: -3
Incrementing: -2
Decrementing: -3
Incrementing: -2
Incrementing: -1
Incrementing: 0
Arithmetic complete.
```

You'll notice that we always call Unlock within a defer statement. This is a very common idiom when utilizing a Mutex to ensure the call always happens, even when
panicing. Failing to do so will probably cause your program to deadlock.

Critical sections are so named because they reflect a bottleneck in your program. It is
somewhat expensive to enter and exit a critical section, and so generally people
attempt to minimize the time spent in critical sections.

One strategy for doing so is to reduce the cross-section of the critical section. There
may be memory that needs to be shared between multiple concurrent processes, but
perhaps not all of these processes will read *and* write to this memory. If this is the
case, you can take advantage of a different type of mutex: sync.RWMutex.

The sync.RWMutex is conceptually the same thing as a Mutex: it guards access to
memory; however, RWMutex gives you a little bit more control over the memory. You

can request a lock for reading, in which case you will be granted access unless the lock is being held for writing. This means that an arbitrary number of readers can hold a reader lock so long as nothing else is holding a writer lock. Here's an example that demonstrates a producer that is less active than the numerous consumers the code creates:

```go
producer := func(wg *sync.WaitGroup, l sync.Locker) { ❶
    defer wg.Done()
    for i := 5; i > 0; i-- {
        l.Lock()
        l.Unlock()
        time.Sleep(1) ❷
    }
}

observer := func(wg *sync.WaitGroup, l sync.Locker) {
    defer wg.Done()
    l.Lock()
    defer l.Unlock()
}

test := func(count int, mutex, rwMutex sync.Locker) time.Duration {
    var wg sync.WaitGroup
    wg.Add(count+1)
    beginTestTime := time.Now()
    go producer(&wg, mutex)
    for i := count; i > 0; i-- {
        go observer(&wg, rwMutex)
    }

    wg.Wait()
    return time.Since(beginTestTime)
}

tw := tabwriter.NewWriter(os.Stdout, 0, 1, 2, ' ', 0)
defer tw.Flush()

var m sync.RWMutex
fmt.Fprintf(tw, "Readers\tRWMutext\tMutex\n")
for i := 0; i < 20; i++ {
    count := int(math.Pow(2, float64(i)))
    fmt.Fprintf(
        tw,
        "%d\t%v\t%v\n",
        count,
        test(count, &m, m.RLocker()),
        test(count, &m, &m),
    )
}
```

❶ The producer function's second parameter is of the type sync.Locker. This interface has two methods, Lock and Unlock, which the Mutex and RWMutex types satisfy.

❷ Here we make the producer sleep for one second to make it less active than the observer goroutines.

This produces:

```
Readers  RWMutext      Mutex
1        38.343µs      15.854µs
2        21.86µs       13.2µs
4        31.01µs       31.358µs
8        63.835µs      24.584µs
16       52.451µs      78.153µs
32       75.569µs      69.492µs
64       141.708µs     163.43µs
128      176.35µs      157.143µs
256      234.808µs     237.182µs
512      262.186µs     434.625µs
1024     459.349µs     850.601µs
2048     840.753µs     1.663279ms
4096     1.683672ms    2.42148ms
8192     2.167814ms    4.13665ms
16384    4.973842ms    8.197173ms
32768    9.236067ms    16.247469ms
65536    16.767161ms   30.948295ms
131072   71.457282ms   62.203475ms
262144   158.76261ms   119.634601ms
524288   303.865661ms  231.072729ms
```

You can see for this particular example that reducing the cross-section of our critical-section really only begins to pay off around 2^{13} readers. This will vary depending on what your critical section is doing, but it's usually advisable to use RWMutex instead of Mutex when it logically makes sense.

Cond

The comment for the Cond type really does a great job of describing its purpose:

> ...a rendezvous point for goroutines waiting for or announcing the occurrence of an event.

In that definition, an "event" is any arbitrary signal between two or more goroutines that carries no information other than the fact that it has occurred. Very often you'll want to wait for one of these signals before continuing execution on a goroutine. If we were to look at how to accomplish this without the Cond type, one naive approach to doing this is to use an infinite loop:

```
for conditionTrue() == false {
}
```

However this would consume all cycles of one core. To fix that, we could introduce a time.Sleep:

```
for conditionTrue() == false {
    time.Sleep(1*time.Millisecond)
}
```

This is better, but it's still inefficient, and you have to figure out how long to sleep for: too long, and you're artificially degrading performance; too short, and you're unnecessarily consuming too much CPU time. It would be better if there were some kind of way for a goroutine to efficiently sleep until it was signaled to wake and check its condition. This is exactly what the Cond type does for us. Using a Cond, we could write the previous examples like this:

```
c := sync.NewCond(&sync.Mutex{}) ❶
c.L.Lock() ❷
for conditionTrue() == false {
    c.Wait() ❸
}
c.L.Unlock() ❹
```

❶ Here we instantiate a new Cond. The NewCond function takes in a type that satisfies the sync.Locker interface. This is what allows the Cond type to facilitate coordination with other goroutines in a concurrent-safe way.

❷ Here we lock the Locker for this condition. This is necessary because the call to Wait automatically calls Unlock on the Locker when entered.

❸ Here we wait to be notified that the condition has occurred. This is a blocking call and the goroutine will be suspended.

❹ Here we unlock the Locker for this condition. This is necessary because when the call to Wait exits, it calls Lock on the Locker for the condition.

This approach is *much* more efficient. Note that the call to Wait doesn't just block, it *suspends* the current goroutine, allowing other goroutines to run on the OS thread. A few other things happen when you call Wait: upon entering Wait, Unlock is called on the Cond variable's Locker, and upon exiting Wait, Lock is called on the Cond variable's Locker. In my opinion, this takes a little getting used to; it's effectively a hidden side effect of the method. It looks like we're holding this lock the entire time while we wait for the condition to occur, but that's not actually the case. When you're scanning code, you'll just have to keep an eye out for this pattern.

Let's expand on this example and show both sides of the equation: a goroutine that is waiting for a signal, and a goroutine that is sending signals. Say we have a queue of fixed length 2, and 10 items we want to push onto the queue. We want to enqueue items as soon as there is room, so we want to be notified as soon as there's room in the queue. Let's try using a Cond to manage this coordination:

```go
c := sync.NewCond(&sync.Mutex{})  ❶
queue := make([]interface{}, 0, 10)  ❷

removeFromQueue := func(delay time.Duration) {
    time.Sleep(delay)
    c.L.Lock()  ❽
    queue = queue[1:]  ❾
    fmt.Println("Removed from queue")
    c.L.Unlock()  ❿
    c.Signal()  ⓫
}

for i := 0; i < 10; i++{
    c.L.Lock()  ❸
    for len(queue) == 2 {  ❹
        c.Wait()  ❺
    }
    fmt.Println("Adding to queue")
    queue = append(queue, struct{}{})
    go removeFromQueue(1*time.Second)  ❻
    c.L.Unlock()  ❼
}
```

❶ First, we create our condition using a standard sync.Mutex as the Locker.

❷ Next, we create a slice with a length of zero. Since we know we'll eventually add 10 items, we instantiate it with a capacity of 10.

❸ We enter the critical section for the condition by calling Lock on the condition's Locker.

❹ Here we check the length of the queue in a loop. This is important because a signal on the condition doesn't necessarily mean what you've been waiting for has occurred—only that *something* has occurred.

❺ We call Wait, which will suspend the main goroutine until a signal on the condition has been sent.

❻ Here we create a new goroutine that will dequeue an element after one second.

❼ Here we exit the condition's critical section since we've successfully enqueued an item.

❽ We once again enter the critical section for the condition so we can modify data pertinent to the condition.

❾ Here we simulate dequeuing an item by reassigning the head of the slice to the second item.

❿ Here we exit the condition's critical section since we've successfully dequeued an item.

⓫ Here we let a goroutine waiting on the condition know that something has occurred.

This produces:

```
Adding to queue
Adding to queue
Removed from queue
Adding to queue
Removed from queue
Adding to queue
Removed from queue
Adding to queue
Removed from queue
Adding to queue
Removed from queue
Adding to queue
Removed from queue
Adding to queue
Removed from queue
Adding to queue
Removed from queue
Adding to queue
```

As you can see, the program successfully adds all 10 items to the queue (and exits before it has a chance to dequeue the last two items). It also always waits until at least one item is dequeued before enqueing another.

We also have a new method in this example, Signal. This is one of two methods that the Cond type provides for notifying goroutines blocked on a Wait call that the condition has been triggered. The other is a method called Broadcast. Internally, the runtime maintains a FIFO list of goroutines waiting to be signaled; Signal finds the goroutine that's been waiting the longest and notifies that, whereas Broadcast sends a signal to *all* goroutines that are waiting. Broadcast is arguably the more interesting of the two methods as it provides a way to communicate with multiple goroutines at once. We can trivially reproduce Signal with channels (as we'll see in the section

"Channels" on page 64), but reproducing the behavior of repeated calls to Broadcast would be more difficult. In addition, the Cond type is much more performant than utilizing channels.

To get a feel for what it's like to use Broadcast, let's imagine we're creating a GUI application with a button on it. We want to register an arbitrary number of functions that will run when that button is clicked. A Cond is perfect for this because we can use its Broadcast method to notify all registered handlers. Let's see how that might look:

```go
type Button struct { ❶
    Clicked *sync.Cond
}
button := Button{ Clicked: sync.NewCond(&sync.Mutex{}) }

subscribe := func(c *sync.Cond, fn func()) { ❷
    var goroutineRunning sync.WaitGroup
    goroutineRunning.Add(1)
    go func() {
        goroutineRunning.Done()
        c.L.Lock()
        defer c.L.Unlock()
        c.Wait()
        fn()
    }()
    goroutineRunning.Wait()
}

var clickRegistered sync.WaitGroup ❸
clickRegistered.Add(3)
subscribe(button.Clicked, func() { ❹
    fmt.Println("Maximizing window.")
    clickRegistered.Done()
})
subscribe(button.Clicked, func() { ❺
    fmt.Println("Displaying annoying dialog box!")
    clickRegistered.Done()
})
subscribe(button.Clicked, func() { ❻
    fmt.Println("Mouse clicked.")
    clickRegistered.Done()
})

button.Clicked.Broadcast() ❼

clickRegistered.Wait()
```

❶ We define a type Button that contains a condition, Clicked.

❷ Here we define a convenience function that will allow us to register functions to handle signals from a condition. Each handler is run on its own goroutine, and `subscribe` will not exit until that goroutine is confirmed to be running.

❸ Here we set a handler for when the mouse button is raised. It in turn calls `Broad cast` on the `Clicked` `Cond` to let all handlers know that the mouse button has been clicked (a more robust implementation would first check that it had been depressed).

❹ Here we create a `WaitGroup`. This is done only to ensure our program doesn't exit before our writes to `stdout` occur.

❺ Here we register a handler that simulates maximizing the button's window when the button is clicked.

❻ Here we register a handler that simulates displaying a dialog box when the mouse is clicked.

❼ Next, we simulate a user raising the mouse button from having clicked the application's button.

This produces:

```
Mouse clicked.
Maximizing window.
Displaying annoying dialog box!
```

You can see that with one call to `Broadcast` on the `Clicked` `Cond`, all three handlers are run. Were it not for the `clickRegistered` `WaitGroup`, we could call `button.Clicked.Broadcast()` multiple times, and each time all three handlers would be invoked. This is something channels can't do easily and thus is one of the main reasons to utilize the `Cond` type.

Like most other things in the `sync` package, usage of `Cond` works best when constrained to a tight scope, or exposed to a broader scope through a type that encapsulates it.

Once

What do you think this code will print out?

```
var count int

increment := func() {
    count++
}
```

```
var once sync.Once

var increments sync.WaitGroup
increments.Add(100)
for i := 0; i < 100; i++ {
    go func() {
        defer increments.Done()
        once.Do(increment)
    }()
}

increments.Wait()
fmt.Printf("Count is %d\n", count)
```

It's tempting to say the result will be Count is 100, but I'm sure you've noticed the sync.Once variable, and that we're somehow wrapping the call to increment within the Do method of once. In fact, this code will print out the following:

```
Count is 1
```

As the name implies, sync.Once is a type that utilizes some sync primitives internally to ensure that only one call to Do ever calls the function passed in—even on different goroutines. This is indeed because we wrap the call to increment in a sync.Once Do method.

It may seem like the ability to call a function exactly once is a strange thing to encapsulate and put into the standard package, but it turns out that the need for this pattern comes up rather frequently. Just for fun, let's check Go's standard library and see how often Go itself uses this primitive. Here's a grep command that will perform the search:

```
grep -ir sync.Once $(go env GOROOT)/src |wc -l
```

This produces:

```
70
```

There are a few things to note about utilizing sync.Once. Let's take a look at another example; what do you think it will print?

```
var count int
increment := func() { count++ }
decrement := func() { count-- }

var once sync.Once
once.Do(increment)
once.Do(decrement)

fmt.Printf("Count: %d\n", count)
```

This produces:

```
Count: 1
```

Is it surprising that the output displays 1 and not 0? This is because sync.Once only counts the number of times Do is called, not how many times unique functions passed into Do are called. In this way, copies of sync.Once are tightly coupled to the functions they are intended to be called with; once again we see how usage of the types within the sync package work best within a tight scope. I recommend that you formalize this coupling by wrapping any usage of sync.Once in a small lexical block: either a small function, or by wrapping both in a type. What about this example? What do you think will happen?

```
var onceA, onceB sync.Once
var initB func()
initA := func() { onceB.Do(initB) }
initB = func() { onceA.Do(initA) } ❶
onceA.Do(initA) ❷
```

❶ This call can't proceed until the call at ❷ returns.

This program will deadlock because the call to Do at ❶ won't proceed until the call to Do at ❷ exits—a classic example of a deadlock. For some, this may be slightly counterintuitive since it appears as though we're using sync.Once as intended to guard against multiple initialization, but the only thing sync.Once guarantees is that your functions are only called once. Sometimes this is done by deadlocking your program and exposing the flaw in your logic—in this case a circular reference.

Pool

Pool is a concurrent-safe implementation of the object pool pattern. A complete explanation of the object pool pattern is best left to literature on design patterns[2]; however, since Pool resides in the sync package, we'll briefly discuss why you might be interested in utilizing it.

At a high level, a the pool pattern is a way to create and make available a fixed number, or pool, of things for use. It's commonly used to constrain the creation of things that are expensive (e.g., database connections) so that only a fixed number of them are ever created, but an indeterminate number of operations can still request access to these things. In the case of Go's sync.Pool, this data type can be safely used by multiple goroutines.

Pool's primary interface is its Get method. When called, Get will first check whether there are any available instances within the pool to return to the caller, and if not, call its New member variable to create a new one. When finished, callers call Put to place

---

2 Personally, I recommend O'Reilly's excellent book, *Head First Design Patterns*.

the instance they were working with back in the pool for use by other processes. Here's a simple example to demonstrate:

```
myPool := &sync.Pool{
    New: func() interface{} {
        fmt.Println("Creating new instance.")
        return struct{}{}
    },
}

myPool.Get() ❶
instance := myPool.Get() ❶
myPool.Put(instance) ❷
myPool.Get() ❸
```

❶ Here we call Get on the pool. These calls will invoke the New function defined on the pool since instances haven't yet been instantiated.

❷ Here we put an instance previously retrieved back in the pool. This increases the available number of instances to one.

❸ When this call is executed, we will reuse the instance previously allocated and put it back in the pool. The New function will not be invoked.

As we can see, we only see two calls to the New function:

```
Creating new instance.
Creating new instance.
```

So why use a pool and not just instantiate objects as you go? Go has a garbage collector, so the instantiated objects will be automatically cleaned up. What's the point? Consider this example:

```
var numCalcsCreated int
calcPool := &sync.Pool {
    New: func() interface{} {
        numCalcsCreated += 1
        mem := make([]byte, 1024)
        return &mem ❶
    },
}

// Seed the pool with 4KB
calcPool.Put(calcPool.New())
calcPool.Put(calcPool.New())
calcPool.Put(calcPool.New())
calcPool.Put(calcPool.New())

const numWorkers = 1024*1024
var wg sync.WaitGroup
wg.Add(numWorkers)
```

```
for i := numWorkers; i > 0; i-- {
    go func() {
        defer wg.Done()

        mem := calcPool.Get().(*[]byte) ❷
        defer calcPool.Put(mem)

        // Assume something interesting, but quick is being done with
        // this memory.
    }()
}

wg.Wait()
fmt.Printf("%d calculators were created.", numCalcsCreated)
```

❶ Notice that we are storing the *address* of the slice of bytes.

❷ And here we are asserting the type is a pointer to a slice of bytes.

This produces:

```
8 calculators were created.
```

Had I run this example without a sync.Pool, though the results are non-deterministic, in the worst case I could have been attempting to allocate a gigabyte of memory, but as you see from the output, I've only allocated 4 KB.

Another common situation where a Pool is useful is for warming a cache of pre-allocated objects for operations that must run as quickly as possible. In this case, instead of trying to guard the host machine's memory by constraining the number of objects created, we're trying to guard consumers' time by front-loading the time it takes to get a reference to another object. This is very common when writing high-throughput network servers that attempt to respond to requests as quickly as possible. Let's take a look at such a scenario.

First, let's create a function that simulates creating a connection to a service. We'll make this connection take a long time:

```
func connectToService() interface{} {
    time.Sleep(1*time.Second)
    return struct{}{}
}
```

Next, let's see how performant a network service would be if for every request we started a new connection to the service. We'll write a network handler that opens a connection to another service for every connection the network handler accepts. To make the benchmarking simple, we'll only allow one connection at a time:

```
func startNetworkDaemon() *sync.WaitGroup {
    var wg sync.WaitGroup
    wg.Add(1)
```

```
        go func() {
            server, err := net.Listen("tcp", "localhost:8080")
            if err != nil {
                log.Fatalf("cannot listen: %v", err)
            }
            defer server.Close()

            wg.Done()

            for {
                conn, err := server.Accept()
                if err != nil {
                    log.Printf("cannot accept connection: %v", err)
                    continue
                }
                connectToService()
                fmt.Fprintln(conn, "")
                conn.Close()
            }
        }()
        return &wg
    }
```

Now let's benchmark this:

```
    func init() {
        daemonStarted := startNetworkDaemon()
        daemonStarted.Wait()
    }

    func BenchmarkNetworkRequest(b *testing.B) {
        for i := 0; i < b.N; i++ {
            conn, err := net.Dial("tcp", "localhost:8080")
            if err != nil {
                b.Fatalf("cannot dial host: %v", err)
            }
            if _, err := ioutil.ReadAll(conn); err != nil {
                b.Fatalf("cannot read: %v", err)
            }
            conn.Close()
        }
    }

    cd src/gos-concurrency-building-blocks/the-sync-package/pool/ && \
    go test -benchtime=10s -bench=.
```

This produces:

```
BenchmarkNetworkRequest-8        10                          1000385643     ns/op
PASS
ok                               command-line-arguments      11.008s
```

Looks like like roughly 1E9 ns/op. This seems reasonable as far as performance goes, but let's see if we can improve it by using a `sync.Pool` to host connections to our fictitious service:

```go
func warmServiceConnCache() *sync.Pool {
    p := &sync.Pool {
        New: connectToService,
    }
    for i := 0; i < 10; i++ {
        p.Put(p.New())
    }
    return p
}

func startNetworkDaemon() *sync.WaitGroup {
    var wg sync.WaitGroup
    wg.Add(1)
    go func() {
        connPool := warmServiceConnCache()

        server, err := net.Listen("tcp", "localhost:8080")
        if err != nil {
            log.Fatalf("cannot listen: %v", err)
        }
        defer server.Close()

        wg.Done()

        for {
            conn, err := server.Accept()
            if err != nil {
                log.Printf("cannot accept connection: %v", err)
                continue
            }
            svcConn := connPool.Get()
            fmt.Fprintln(conn, "")
            connPool.Put(svcConn)
            conn.Close()
        }
    }()
    return &wg
}
```

And if we benchmark this, like so:

```
cd src/gos-concurrency-building-blocks/the-sync-package/pool && \
go test -benchtime=10s -bench=.
```

We get:

```
BenchmarkNetworkRequest-8          5000                    2904307      ns/op
PASS
ok                        command-line-arguments           32.647s
```

2.9E6 ns/op: three orders of magnitude faster! You can see how utilizing this pattern when working with things that are expensive to create can drastically improve response time.

As we've seen, the object pool design pattern is best used either when you have concurrent processes that require objects, but dispose of them very rapidly after instantiation, or when construction of these objects could negatively impact memory.

However, there is one thing to be wary of when determining whether or not you should utilize a Pool: if the code that utilizes the Pool requires things that are not roughly homogenous, you may spend more time converting what you've retrieved from the Pool than it would have taken to just instantiate it in the first place. For instance, if your program requires slices of random and variable length, a Pool isn't going to help you much. The probability that you'll receive a slice the length you require is low.

So when working with a Pool, just remember the following points:

- When instantiating sync.Pool, give it a New member variable that is thread-safe when called.
- When you receive an instance from Get, make no assumptions regarding the state of the object you receive back.
- Make sure to call Put when you're finished with the object you pulled out of the pool. Otherwise, the Pool is useless. Usually this is done with defer.
- Objects in the pool must be roughly uniform in makeup.

Channels

Channels are one of the synchronization primitives in Go derived from Hoare's CSP. While they can be used to synchronize access of the memory, they are best used to communicate information between goroutines. As we discussed in "Go's Philosophy on Concurrency" on page 31, channels are extremely useful in programs of any size because of their ability to be composed together. After I introduce the channel in this section, we'll explore that composition in the next section, "The select Statement" on page 78.

Like a river, a channel serves as a conduit for a stream of information; values may be passed along the channel, and then read out downstream. For this reason I usually end my chan variable names with the word "Stream." When using channels, you'll pass a value into a chan variable, and then somewhere else in your program read it off the channel. The disparate parts of your program don't require knowledge of each other, only a reference to the same place in memory where the channel resides. This can be done by passing references of channels around your program.

Creating a channel is very simple. Here's an example that expands the creation of a channel out into its declaration and subsequent instantiation so that you can see what both look like. As with other values in Go, you can create channels in one step with the := operator, but you will need to declare channels often, so it's useful to see the two split into individual steps:

```
var dataStream chan interface{}  ❶
dataStream = make(chan interface{})  ❷
```

❶ Here we declare a channel. We say it is "of type" interface{} since the type we've declared is the empty interface.

❷ Here we instantiate the channel using the built-in make function.

This example defines a channel, dataStream, upon which any value can be written or read (because we used the empty interface). Channels can also be declared to only support a unidirectional flow of data—that is, you can define a channel that only supports sending or receiving information. I'll explain why this is important later in this section.

To declare a unidirectional channel, you'll simply include the <- operator. To both declare and instantiate a channel that can only read, place the <- operator on the left-hand side, like so:

```
var dataStream <-chan interface{}
dataStream := make(<-chan interface{})
```

And to declare and create a channel that can only send, you place the <- operator on the righthand side, like so:

```
var dataStream chan<- interface{}
dataStream := make(chan<- interface{})
```

You don't often see unidirectional channels instantiated, but you'll often see them used as function parameters and return types, which is very useful, as we'll see. This is possible because Go will implicitly convert bidirectional channels to unidirectional channels when needed. Here's an example:

```
var receiveChan <-chan interface{}
var sendChan chan<- interface{}
dataStream := make(chan interface{})

// Valid statements:
receiveChan = dataStream
sendChan = dataStream
```

Keep in mind channels are typed. In this example, we created a chan interface{} variable, which means that we can place any kind of data onto it, but we can also give it a stricter type to constrain the type of data it could pass along. Here's an example of a channel for integers; I'm also going to switch to the more canonical way of instantiating channels for brevity now that we're past the introduction:

```
intStream := make(chan int)
```

To use channels, we'll once again make use of the <- operator. Sending is done by placing the <- operator to the right of a channel, and receiving is done by placing the <- operator to the left of the channel. Another way to think of this is the data flows into the variable in the direction the arrow points. Let's take a look at a simple example:

```
stringStream := make(chan string)
go func() {
    stringStream <- "Hello channels!" ❶
}()
fmt.Println(<-stringStream) ❷
```

❶ Here we pass a string literal onto the channel stringStream.

❷ Here we read the string literal off of the channel and print it out to stdout.

This produces:

```
Hello channels!
```

Pretty simple, right? All you need is a channel variable and you can pass data onto it and read data off of it; however, it is an error to try and write a value onto a read-only channel, and an error to read a value from a write-only channel. If we try and compile the following example, Go's compiler will let us know that we're doing something illegal:

```
writeStream := make(chan<- interface{})
readStream := make(<-chan interface{})

<-writeStream
readStream <- struct{}{}
```

This will error with:

```
invalid operation: <-writeStream (receive from send-only type
  chan<- interface {})
invalid operation: readStream <- struct {} literal (send to receive-only
  type <-chan interface {})
```

This is part of Go's type system that allows us type-safety even when dealing with concurrency primitives. As we'll see later in this section, this is a powerful way to make declarations about our API and to build composable, logical programs that are easy to reason about.

Recall that earlier in the chapter we highlighted the fact that just because a goroutine was scheduled, there was no guarantee that it would run before the process exited; yet the previous example is complete and correct with no code omitted. You may have been wondering why the anonymous goroutine completes before the main goroutine does; did I just get lucky when I ran this? Let's take a brief digression to explore this.

This example works because channels in Go are said to be *blocking*. This means that any goroutine that attempts to write to a channel that is full will wait until the channel has been emptied, and any goroutine that attempts to read from a channel that is empty will wait until at least one item is placed on it. In this example, our fmt.Println contains a pull from the channel stringStream and will sit there until a value is placed on the channel. Likewise, the anonymous goroutine is attempting to place a string literal on the stringStream, and so the goroutine will not exit until the write is successful. Thus, the main goroutine and the anonymous goroutine block deterministically.

This can cause deadlocks if you don't structure your program correctly. Take a look at the following example, which introduces a nonsensical conditional to prevent the anonymous goroutine from placing a value on the channel:

```
stringStream := make(chan string)
go func() {
    if 0 != 1 { ❶
        return
    }
    stringStream <- "Hello channels!"
}()
fmt.Println(<-stringStream)
```

❶ Here we ensure the stringStream channel never gets a value placed upon it.

This will panic with:

```
fatal error: all goroutines are asleep - deadlock!

goroutine 1 [chan receive]:
main.main()
```

```
    /tmp/babel-23079IVB/go-src-230795Jc.go:15 +0x97
exit status 2
```

The main goroutine is waiting for a value to be placed onto the `stringStream` channel, and because of our conditional, this will never happen. When the anonymous goroutine exits, Go correctly detects that all goroutines are asleep, and reports a deadlock. Later in this section, I'll explain how to structure our programs as a first step toward preventing deadlocks like this, and in the next chapter how to prevent these altogether. In the meantime, let's get back to discussing reading from channels.

The receiving form of the `<-` operator can also optionally return two values, like so:

```
stringStream := make(chan string)
go func() {
    stringStream <- "Hello channels!"
}()
salutation, ok := <-stringStream  ❶
fmt.Printf("(%v): %v", ok, salutation)
```

❶ Here we receive both a string, `salutation`, and a boolean, ok.

This will produce:

```
(true): Hello channels!
```

Very curious! What does the boolean signify? The second return value is a way for a read operation to indicate whether the read off the channel was a value generated by a write elsewhere in the process, or a default value generated from a closed channel. Wait a second; a closed channel, what's that?

In programs, it's very useful to be able to indicate that no more values will be sent over a channel. This helps downstream processes know when to move on, exit, re-open communications on a new or different channel, etc. We could accomplish this with a special sentinel value for each type, but this would duplicate the effort for all developers, and it's really a function of the channel and not the data type, so closing a channel is like a universal sentinel that says, "Hey, upstream isn't going to be writing any more values, do what you will." To close a channel, we use the `close` keyword, like so:

```
valueStream := make(chan interface{})
close(valueStream)
```

Interestingly, we can read from a closed channel as well. Take this example:

```
intStream := make(chan int)
close(intStream)
integer, ok := <- intStream  ❶
fmt.Printf("(%v): %v", ok, integer)
```

❶ Here we read from a closed stream.

This will produce:

```
(false): 0
```

Notice that we never placed anything on this channel; we closed it immediately. We were still able to perform a read operation, and in fact, we could continue performing reads on this channel indefinitely despite the channel remaining closed. This is to allow support for multiple downstream reads from a single upstream writer on the channel (in Chapter 4 we'll see that this is a common scenario). The second value returned—here stored in the ok variable—is false, indicating that the value we received is the zero value for int, or 0, and not a value placed on the stream.

This opens up a few new patterns for us. The first is *ranging* over a channel. The range keyword—used in conjunction with the for statement—supports channels as arguments, and will automatically break the loop when a channel is closed. This allows for concise iteration over the values on a channel. Let's take a look at an example:

```
intStream := make(chan int)
go func() {
    defer close(intStream) ❶
    for i := 1; i <= 5; i++ {
        intStream <- i
    }
}()

for integer := range intStream { ❷
    fmt.Printf("%v ", integer)
}
```

❶ Here we ensure that the channel is closed before we exit the goroutine. This is a very common pattern.

❷ Here we range over intStream.

As you can see, all the values are printed out and then the program exits:

```
1 2 3 4 5
```

Notice how the loop doesn't need an exit criteria, and the range does not return the second boolean value. The specifics of handling a closed channel are managed for you to keep the loop concise.

Closing a channel is also one of the ways you can signal multiple goroutines simultaneously. If you have n goroutines waiting on a single channel, instead of writing n times to the channel to unblock each goroutine, you can simply close the channel. Since a closed channel can be read from an infinite number of times, it doesn't matter how many goroutines are waiting on it, and closing the channel is both cheaper and faster than performing n writes. Here's an example of unblocking multiple goroutines at once:

```
begin := make(chan interface{})
var wg sync.WaitGroup
for i := 0; i < 5; i++ {
    wg.Add(1)
    go func(i int) {
        defer wg.Done()
        <-begin ❶
        fmt.Printf("%v has begun\n", i)
    }(i)
}

fmt.Println("Unblocking goroutines...")
close(begin) ❷
wg.Wait()
```

❶ Here the goroutine waits until it is told it can continue.

❷ Here we close the channel, thus unblocking all the goroutines simultaneously.

You can see that none of the goroutines begin to run until after we close the begin channel:

```
Unblocking goroutines...
4 has begun
2 has begun
3 has begun
0 has begun
1 has begun
```

Remember in "The sync Package" on page 47 we discussed using the sync.Cond type to perform the same behavior. You can certainly use that, but as we've discussed, channels are composable, so this is my favorite way to unblock multiple goroutines at the same time.

We can also create *buffered channels*, which are channels that are given a *capacity* when they're instantiated. This means that even if no reads are performed on the channel, a goroutine can still perform n writes, where n is the capacity of the buffered channel. Here's how to declare and instantiate one:

```
var dataStream chan interface{}
dataStream = make(chan interface{}, 4) ❶
```

❶ Here we create a buffered channel with a capacity of four. This means that we can place four things onto the channel regardless of whether it's being read from.

Once again, I've exploded out the instantiation into two lines so you can see that the declaration of a buffered channel is no different than an unbuffered one. This is somewhat interesting because it means that the goroutine that instantiates a channel controls whether it's buffered. This suggests that the creation of a channel should probably be tightly coupled to goroutines that will be performing writes on it so that we can reason about its behavior and performance more easily. We'll come back to this later in this section.

Unbuffered channels are also defined in terms of buffered channels: an unbuffered channel is simply a buffered channel created with a capacity of 0. Here's an example of two channels that have equivalent functionality:

```
a := make(chan int)
b := make(chan int, 0)
```

Both channels are int channels with a capacity of zero. Remember that when we discussed blocking, we said that writes to a channel block if a channel is full, and reads from a channel block if the channel is empty? "Full" and "empty" are functions of the capacity, or buffer size. An unbuffered channel has a capacity of zero and so it's already full before any writes. A buffered channel with no receivers and a capacity of four would be full after four writes, and block on the fifth write since it has nowhere else to place the fifth element. Like unbuffered channels, buffered channels are still blocking; the preconditions that the channel be empty or full are just different. In this way, buffered channels are an in-memory FIFO queue for concurrent processes to communicate over.

To help understand this, let's illustrate what's happening in our example of a buffered channel with a capacity of four. First, let's initialize it:

```
c := make(chan rune, 4)
```

Logically, this creates a channel with a buffer that has four slots, like so:

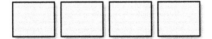

Now, let's write to the channel:

```
c <- 'A'
```

When this channel has no readers, the A rune will be placed in the first slot in the channel's buffer, like so:

Each subsequent write onto the buffered channel (again, assuming no readers) would fill up the remaining slots in the buffered channel, like so:

```
c <- 'B'
```

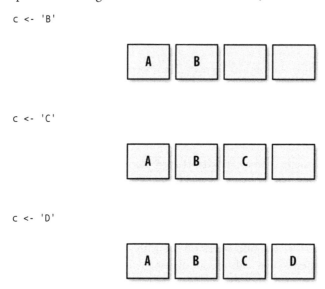

```
c <- 'C'
```

```
c <- 'D'
```

After four writes, our buffered channel with a capacity of four is full. What happens if we attempt to write to the channel again?

```
c <- 'E'
```

The goroutine performing this write is blocked! The goroutine will remain blocked until room is made in the buffer by some goroutine performing a read. Let's see what that looks like:

```
<-c
```

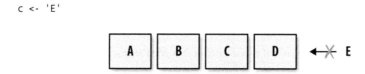

As you can see, the read receives the first rune that was placed on the channel, A, the write that was blocked becomes unblocked, and E is placed on the end of the buffer.

It also bears mentioning that if a buffered channel is empty and has a receiver, the buffer will be bypassed and the value will be passed directly from the sender to the receiver. In practice, this happens transparently, but it's worth knowing for understanding the performance profile of buffered channels.

Buffered channels can be useful in certain situations, but you should create them with care. As we'll see in the next chapter, buffered channels can easily become a premature optimization and also hide deadlocks by making them more unlikely to happen. This sounds like a good thing, but I'm guessing you'd much rather find a deadlock while writing code the first time, and not in the middle of the night when your production system goes down.

Let's examine another, more complete code example that uses buffered channels just so you can get a better idea of what they're like to work with:

```
var stdoutBuff bytes.Buffer ❶
defer stdoutBuff.WriteTo(os.Stdout) ❷

intStream := make(chan int, 4) ❸
go func() {
    defer close(intStream)
    defer fmt.Fprintln(&stdoutBuff, "Producer Done.")
    for i := 0; i < 5; i++ {
        fmt.Fprintf(&stdoutBuff, "Sending: %d\n", i)
        intStream <- i
    }
}()

for integer := range intStream {
    fmt.Fprintf(&stdoutBuff, "Received %v.\n", integer)
}
```

❶ Here we create an in-memory buffer to help mitigate the nondeterministic nature of the output. It doesn't give us any guarantees, but it's a little faster than writing to stdout directly.

❷ Here we ensure that the buffer is written out to stdout before the process exits.

❸ Here we create a buffered channel with a capacity of one.

In this example, the order in which output to stdout is written is nondeterministic, but you can still get a rough idea of how the anonymous goroutine is working. If you look at the output, you can see how our anonymous goroutine is able to place all five of its results on the intStream and exit before the main goroutine pulls even one result off:

```
Sending: 0
Sending: 1
Sending: 2
Sending: 3
Sending: 4
```

```
Producer Done.
Received 0.
Received 1.
Received 2.
Received 3.
Received 4.
```

This is an example of an optimization that can be useful under the right conditions: if a goroutine making writes to a channel has knowledge of how many writes it will make, it can be useful to create a buffered channel whose capacity is the number of writes to be made, and then make those writes as quickly as possible. There are, of course, caveats, and we'll cover them in the next chapter.

We've discussed unbuffered channels, buffered channels, bidirectional channels, and unidirectional channels. The only aspect of channels we haven't covered is the default value for channels: nil. How do programs interact with a nil channel? First, let's try reading from a nil channel:

```
var dataStream chan interface{}
<-dataStream
```

This panics with:

```
fatal error: all goroutines are asleep - deadlock!

goroutine 1 [chan receive (nil chan)]:
main.main()
    /tmp/babel-23079IVB/go-src-2307904q.go:9 +0x3f
exit status 2
```

A deadlock! This indicates that reading from a nil channel will block (although not necessarily deadlock) a program. What about writes?

```
var dataStream chan interface{}
dataStream <- struct{}{}
```

This produces:

```
fatal error: all goroutines are asleep - deadlock!

goroutine 1 [chan send (nil chan)]:
main.main()
    /tmp/babel-23079IVB/go-src-23079dnD.go:9 +0x77
exit status 2
```

It looks like writes to a nil channel will also block. That just leaves one operation, close. What happens if we attempt to close a nil channel?

```
var dataStream chan interface{}
close(dataStream)
```

This produces:

```
panic: close of nil channel

goroutine 1 [running]:
panic(0x45b0c0, 0xc42000a160)
    /usr/local/lib/go/src/runtime/panic.go:500 +0x1a1
main.main()
    /tmp/babel-23079IVB/go-src-230794uu.go:9 +0x2a
exit status 2
```

Yipes! This is probably the worst outcome of all the operations performed on a nil channel: a panic. Be sure to ensure the channels you're working with are always initialized first.

We've gone over a lot of rules for how to interact with channels. Now that you understand the how and why of performing operations on channels, let's create a handy reference for what the defined behavior of working with channels is. Table 3-2 enumerates the operations on channels and what will happen given the possible channel states.

Table 3-2. Result of channel operations given a channel's state

Operation	Channel state	Result
Read	nil	Block
	Open and Not Empty	Value
	Open and Empty	Block
	Closed	<default value>, false
	Write Only	Compilation Error
Write	nil	Block
	Open and Full	Block
	Open and Not Full	Write Value
	Closed	**panic**
	Receive Only	Compilation Error
close	nil	**panic**
	Open and Not Empty	Closes Channel; reads succeed until channel is drained, then reads produce default value
	Open and Empty	Closes Channel; reads produces default value
	Closed	**panic**
	Receive Only	Compilation Error

If we examine this table, we see a few areas that could lead to trouble. We have three operations that can cause a goroutine to block, and three operations that can cause your program to panic! At first glance, it looks as though channels might be dangerous to utilize, but after examining the motivation of these results and framing the use of channels, it becomes less scary and begins to make a lot of sense. Let's take a look at how we can organize the different types of channels to begin building something that's robust and stable.

The first thing we should do to put channels in the right context is to assign channel *ownership*. I'll define ownership as being a goroutine that instantiates, writes, and closes a channel. Much like memory in languages without garbage collection, it's important to clarify which goroutine owns a channel in order to reason about our programs logically. Unidirectional channel declarations are the tool that will allow us to distinguish between goroutines that own channels and those that only utilize them: channel owners have a write-access view into the channel (chan or chan<-), and channel utilizers only have a read-only view into the channel (<-chan). Once we make this distinction between channel owners and nonchannel owners, the results from the preceding table follow naturally, and we can begin to assign responsibilities to goroutines that own channels and those that do not.

Let's begin with channel owners. The goroutine that owns a channel should:

1. Instantiate the channel.
2. Perform writes, or pass ownership to another goroutine.
3. Close the channel.
4. Ecapsulate the previous three things in this list and expose them via a reader channel.

By assigning these responsibilities to channel owners, a few things happen:

- Because we're the one initializing the channel, we remove the risk of deadlocking by writing to a nil channel.
- Because we're the one initializing the channel, we remove the risk of panicing by closing a nil channel.
- Because we're the one who decides when the channel gets closed, we remove the risk of panicing by writing to a closed channel.
- Because we're the one who decides when the channel gets closed, we remove the risk of panicing by closing a channel more than once.
- We wield the type checker at compile time to prevent improper writes to our channel.

Now let's look at those blocking operations that can occur when reading. As a consumer of a channel, I only have to worry about two things:

- Knowing when a channel is closed.

- Responsibly handling blocking for any reason.

To address the first point we simply examine the second return value from the read operation, as discussed previously. The second point is much harder to define because it depends on your algorithm: you may want to time out, you may want to stop reading when someone tells you to, or you may just be content to block for the lifetime of the process. The important thing is that as a consumer you should handle the fact that reads can and will block. We'll examine ways to achieve any goal of a channel reader in the next chapter.

For now, let's look at an example to help clarify these concepts. Let's create a goroutine that clearly owns a channel, and a consumer that clearly handles blocking and closing of a channel:

```
chanOwner := func() <-chan int {
    resultStream := make(chan int, 5)  ❶
    go func() {  ❷
        defer close(resultStream)  ❸
        for i := 0; i <= 5; i++ {
            resultStream <- i
        }
    }()
    return resultStream  ❹
}

resultStream := chanOwner()
for result := range resultStream {  ❺
    fmt.Printf("Received: %d\n", result)
}
fmt.Println("Done receiving!")
```

❶ Here we instantiate a buffered channel. Since we know we'll produce six results, we create a buffered channel of five so that the goroutine can complete as quickly as possible.

❷ Here we start an anonymous goroutine that performs writes on `resultStream`. Notice that we've inverted how we create goroutines. It is now encapsulated within the surrounding function.

❸ Here we ensure `resultStream` is closed once we're finished with it. As the channel owner, this is our responsibility.

❹ Here we return the channel. Since the return value is declared as a read-only channel, `resultStream` will implicitly be converted to read-only for consumers.

❺ Here we range over `resultStream`. As a consumer, we are only concerned with blocking and closed channels.

This produces:

```
Received: 0
Received: 1
Received: 2
Received: 3
Received: 4
Received: 5
Done receiving!
```

Notice how the lifecycle of the `resultStream` channel is encapsulated within the `chanOwner` function. It's very clear that the writes will not happen on a nil or closed channel, and that the close will always happen once. This removes a large swath of risk from our program. I highly encourage you to do what you can in your programs to keep the scope of channel ownership small so that these things remain obvious. If you have a channel as a member variable of a struct with numerous methods on it, it's going to quickly become unclear how the channel will behave.

The consumer function only has access to a read channel, and therefore only needs to know how it should handle blocking reads and channel closes. In this small example, we've taken the stance that it's perfectly OK to block the life of the program until the channel is closed.

If you engineer your code to follow this principle, it will be much easier to reason about your system, and it's much more likely it will perform as you expect it to. I can't promise that you'll never introduce deadlocks or panics, but when you do, I think you'll find that the scope of your channel ownership has either gotten too large, or ownership has become unclear.

Channels were one of the things that drew me to Go in the first place. Combined with the simplicity of goroutines and closures, it was apparent to me how easy it would be to write clean, correct, concurrent code. In many ways, channels are the glue that binds goroutines together. This chapter should have given you a good overview of what channels are, and how to use them. The real fun begins when we start composing channels to form higher-order concurrency design patterns. We'll get to that in the next chapter.

The select Statement

The `select` statement is the glue that binds channels together; it's how we're able to compose channels together in a program to form larger abstractions. If channels are the glue that binds goroutines together, what does that say about the `select` statement? It is not an overstatement to say that `select` statements are one of the most crucial things in a Go program with concurrency. You can find `select` statements binding together channels locally, within a single function or type, and also globally, at the intersection of two or more components in a system. In addition to joining components, at these critical junctures in your program, `select` statements can help safely bring channels together with concepts like cancellations, timeouts, waiting, and default values.

Conversely, if `select` statements are the lingua franca of your program, and they exclusively deal with channels, how do you think the components of your program should coordinate with one another? We'll examine this question specifically in Chapter 5 (hint: prefer using channels).

So what are these powerful `select` statements? How do we use them, and how do they work? Let's start by just laying one out. Here's a very simple example:

```
var c1, c2 <-chan interface{}
var c3 chan<- interface{}
select {
case <- c1:
    // Do something
case <- c2:
    // Do something
case c3<- struct{}{}:
    // Do something
}
```

It looks a bit like a `switch` block, doesn't it? Just like a `switch` block, a `select` block encompasses a series of `case` statements that guard a series of statements; however, that's where the similarities end. Unlike `switch` blocks, `case` statements in a `select` block aren't tested sequentially, and execution won't automatically fall through if none of the criteria are met.

Instead, all channel reads and writes are considered simultaneously[3] to see if any of them are ready: populated or closed channels in the case of reads, and channels that are not at capacity in the case of writes. If none of the channels are ready, the entire `select` statement blocks. Then when one the channels is ready, that operation will proceed, and its corresponding statements will execute. Let's take a look at a quick example:

```
start := time.Now()
c := make(chan interface{})
go func() {
    time.Sleep(5*time.Second)
    close(c) ❶
}()

fmt.Println("Blocking on read...")
select {
case <-c: ❷
```

---

3 What's happening under the covers is a bit more complicated, as we'll see in Chapter 6.

```
        fmt.Printf("Unblocked %v later.\n", time.Since(start))
    }
```

❶ Here we close the channel after waiting five seconds.

❷ Here we attempt a read on the channel. Note that as this code is written, we don't require a select statement—we could simply write <-c—but we'll expand on this example.

This produces:

```
Blocking on read...
Unblocked 5.000170047s later.
```

As you can see, we only unblock roughly five seconds after entering the select block. This is a simple and efficient way to block while we're waiting for something to happen, but if we reflect for a moment we can come up with some questions:

- What happens when multiple channels have something to read?
- What if there are never any channels that become ready?
- What if we want to do something but no channels are currently ready?

The first question of multiple channels being ready simultaneously seems interesting. Let's just try it and see what happens!

```
c1 := make(chan interface{}); close(c1)
c2 := make(chan interface{}); close(c2)

var c1Count, c2Count int
for i := 1000; i >= 0; i-- {
    select {
    case <-c1:
        c1Count++
    case <-c2:
        c2Count++
    }
}

fmt.Printf("c1Count: %d\nc2Count: %d\n", c1Count, c2Count)
```

This produces:

```
c1Count: 505
c2Count: 496
```

As you can see, in a thousand iterations, roughly half the time the select statement read from c1, and roughly half the time it read from c2. That seems interesting, and maybe a bit too coincidental. In fact, it is! The Go runtime will perform a pseudo-random uniform selection over the set of case statements. This just means that of your set of case statements, each has an equal chance of being selected as all the others.

This may seem unimportant at first, but the reasoning behind it is incredibly interesting. Let's first make a pretty obvious statement: the Go runtime cannot know anything about the intent of your select statement; that is, it cannot infer your problem space or why you placed a group of channels together into a select statement. Because of this, the best thing the Go runtime can hope to do is to work well in the average case. A good way to do that is to introduce a random variable into your equation—in this case, which channel to select from. By weighting the chance of each channel being utilized equally, all Go programs that utilize the select statement will perform well in the average case.

What about the second question: what happens if there are never any channels that become ready? If there's nothing useful you can do when all the channels are blocked, but you also can't block forever, you may want to time out. Go's time package provides an elegant way to do this with channels that fits nicely within the paradigm of select statements. Here's an example using one:

```
var c <-chan int
select {
case <-c: ❶
case <-time.After(1 * time.Second):
    fmt.Println("Timed out.")
}
```

❶ This case statement will never become unblocked because we're reading from a nil channel.

This produces:

```
Timed out.
```

The time.After function takes in a time.Duration argument and returns a channel that will send the current time after the duration you provide it. This offers a concise way to time out in select statements. We'll revisit this pattern in Chapter 4 where we'll discuss a more robust solution to this problem.

This leaves us the remaining question: what happens when no channel is ready, and we need to do something in the meantime? Like case statements, the select statement also allows for a default clause in case you'd like to do something if all the channels you're selecting against are blocking. Here's an example:

```
start := time.Now()
var c1, c2 <-chan int
select {
case <-c1:
case <-c2:
default:
```

```
        fmt.Printf("In default after %v\n\n", time.Since(start))
    }
```

This produces:

```
In default after 1.421µs
```

You can see that it ran the `default` statement almost instantaneously. This allows you to exit a `select` block without blocking. Usually you'll see a `default` clause used in conjunction with a for-select loop. This allows a goroutine to make progress on work while waiting for another goroutine to report a result. Here's an example of that:

```
done := make(chan interface{})
go func() {
    time.Sleep(5*time.Second)
    close(done)
}()

workCounter := 0
loop:
for {
    select {
    case <-done:
        break loop
    default:
    }

    // Simulate work
    workCounter++
    time.Sleep(1*time.Second)
}

    fmt.Printf("Achieved %v cycles of work before signalled to stop.\n", workCounter)
```

This produces:

```
Achieved 5 cycles of work before signalled to stop.
```

In this case, we have a loop that is doing some kind of work and occasionally checking whether it should stop.

Finally, there is a special case for empty `select` statements: `select` statements with no `case` clauses. These look like this:

```
select {}
```

This statement will simply block forever.

In Chapter 6, we'll take a deeper look into how the `select` statement works. From a higher-level perspective, it should be evident how it can help you compose various concepts and subsystems together safely and efficiently.

The GOMAXPROCS Lever

In the `runtime` package, there is a function called `GOMAXPROCS`. In my opinion, the name is misleading: people often think this function relates to the number of logical processors on the host machine—and in a roundabout way it does—but really this function controls the number of OS threads that will host so-called "work queues." For more information on what this function is and how it works, see Chapter 6.

Prior to Go 1.5, `GOMAXPROCS` was always set to one, and usually you'd find this snippet in most Go programs:

```
runtime.GOMAXPROCS(runtime.NumCPU())
```

Almost universally, developers want to take advantage of all the cores on the machine their process is running in. Because of this, in subsequent Go versions, it is now automatically set to the number of logical CPUs on the host machine.

So why would you want to tweak this value? Most of the time you won't want to. Go's scheduling algorithm is good enough in most situations that increasing or decreasing the number of worker queues and threads will likely do more harm than good, but there are still some situations where changing this value might be useful.

For instance, I worked on one project that had a test suite plagued by race conditions. However it came to be, the team had a handful of packages that had tests that sometimes failed. The infrastructure on which we ran our tests only had four logical CPUs, and so at any one point in time we had four goroutines executing simultaneously. By increasing `GOMAXPROCS` beyond the number of logical CPUs we had, we were able to trigger the race conditions much more often, and thus get them corrected faster.

Others may find through experimentation that their programs run better with a certain number of worker queues and threads, but I urge caution. If you are squeezing out performance by tweaking this, be sure to do so after every commit, when you use different hardware, and when using different versions of Go. Tweaking this value pushes your program closer to the metal it's running on, but at the cost of abstraction and long-term performance stability.

Conclusion

In this chapter, we've covered all the basic concurrency primitives Go provides for your disposal. If you've read and understood this, congratulations! You're well on your way to writing performant, readable, and logically correct programs. You know when it's appropriate to reach for the memory access synchronization primitives in the `sync` package, and when it's more appropriate to "share memory by communicating" using channels and the `select` statement.

All that remains to understand when writing concurrent Go code is how to combine these primitives in structured ways that scale and are easy to understand. In the second half of the book, we'll be looking at how to do just that. The next chapter is all about how to combine these primitives using patterns that the community has discovered.

CHAPTER 4

Concurrency Patterns in Go

We've explored the fundamentals of Go's concurrency primitives and discussed how to properly use these primitives. In this chapter, we'll do a deep-dive into how to compose these primitives into patterns that will help keep your system scalable and maintainable.

However, before we get started, we need to touch upon the format of some of the patterns contained in this chapter. In a lot of the examples, we'll be using channels that pass empty interfaces (`interface{}`) around. Usage of empty interfaces in Go is controversial; however, I've done this for a couple of reasons. The first is that it makes it easier to write concise examples in the remainder of the book. The second is that in some cases I believe this to be more representative of what the pattern is trying to accomplish. We'll discuss this point more directly in the section "Pipelines" on page 100.

If this is just too contentious to you, remember that you can always create Go generators for this code, and generate the patterns to utilize the type you're interested in.

With that said, let's dive in and learn about some patterns for concurrency in Go!

Confinement

When working with concurrent code, there are a few different options for safe operation. We've gone over two of them:

- Synchronization primitives for sharing memory (e.g., `sync.Mutex`)
- Synchronization via communicating (e.g., channels)

However, there are a couple of other options that are implicitly safe within multiple concurrent processes:

- Immutable data
- Data protected by confinement

In some sense, immutable data is ideal because it is implicitly concurrent-safe. Each concurrent process may operate on the same data, but it may not modify it. If it wants to create new data, it must create a new copy of the data with the desired modifications. This allows not only a lighter cognitive load on the developer, but can also lead to faster programs if it leads to smaller critical sections (or eliminates them altogether). In Go, you can achieve this by writing code that utilizes copies of values instead of pointers to values in memory. Some languages support utilization of pointers with explicitly immutable values; however, Go is not among these.

Confinement can also allow for a lighter cognitive load on the developer and smaller critical sections. The techniques to confine concurrent values are a bit more involved than simply passing copies of values, so in this chapter we'll explore these confinement techniques in depth.

Confinement is the simple yet powerful idea of ensuring information is only ever available from *one* concurrent process. When this is achieved, a concurrent program is implicitly safe and no synchronization is needed. There are two kinds of confinement possible: ad hoc and lexical.

Ad hoc confinement is when you achieve confinement through a convention— whether it be set by the languages community, the group you work within, or the codebase you work within. In my opinion, sticking to convention is difficult to achieve on projects of any size unless you have tools to perform static analysis on your code every time someone commits some code. Here's an example of ad hoc confinement that demonstrates why:

```
data := make([]int, 4)

loopData := func(handleData chan<- int) {
    defer close(handleData)
    for i := range data {
        handleData <- data[i]
    }
}

handleData := make(chan int)
go loopData(handleData)

for num := range handleData {
    fmt.Println(num)
}
```

We can see that the data slice of integers is available from both the loopData function and the loop over the handleData channel; however, by convention we're only accessing it from the loopData function. But as the code is touched by many people, and deadlines loom, mistakes might be made, and the confinement might break down and cause issues. As I mentioned, a static-analysis tool might catch these kinds of issues, but static analysis on a Go codebase suggests a level of maturity that not many teams achieve. This is why I prefer lexical confinement: it wields the compiler to enforce the confinement.

Lexical confinement involves using lexical scope to expose only the correct data and concurrency primitives for multiple concurrent processes to use. It makes it impossible to do the wrong thing. We've actually already touched on this topic in Chapter 3. Recall the section on channels, which discusses only exposing read or write aspects of a channel to the concurrent processes that need them. Let's take a look at that example again:

```
chanOwner := func() <-chan int {
    results := make(chan int, 5)  ❶
    go func() {
        defer close(results)
        for i := 0; i <= 5; i++ {
            results <- i
        }
    }()
    return results
}

consumer := func(results <-chan int) {  ❸
    for result := range results {
        fmt.Printf("Received: %d\n", result)
    }
    fmt.Println("Done receiving!")
}

results := chanOwner()          ❷
consumer(results)
```

❶ Here we instantiate the channel within the lexical scope of the chanOwner function. This limits the scope of the write aspect of the results channel to the closure defined below it. In other words, it *confines* the write aspect of this channel to prevent other goroutines from writing to it.

❷ Here we receive the read aspect of the channel and we're able to pass it into the consumer, which can do nothing but read from it. Once again this confines the main goroutine to a read-only view of the channel.

❸ Here we receive a read-only copy of an int channel. By declaring that the only usage we require is read access, we confine usage of the channel within the con sume function to only reads.

Set up this way, it is impossible to utilize the channels in this small example. This is a good lead-in to confinement, but probably not a very interesting example since channels are concurrent-safe. Let's take a look at an example of confinement that uses a data structure which is not concurrent-safe, an instance of bytes.Buffer:

```go
printData := func(wg *sync.WaitGroup, data []byte) {
    defer wg.Done()

    var buff bytes.Buffer
    for _, b := range data {
        fmt.Fprintf(&buff, "%c", b)
    }
    fmt.Println(buff.String())
}

var wg sync.WaitGroup
wg.Add(2)
data := []byte("golang")
go printData(&wg, data[:3])      ❶
go printData(&wg, data[3:])      ❷

wg.Wait()
```

❶ Here we pass in a slice containing the first three bytes in the data structure.

❷ Here we pass in a slice containing the last three bytes in the data structure.

In this example, you can see that because printData doesn't close around the data slice, it cannot access it, and needs to take in a slice of byte to operate on. We pass in different subsets of the slice, thus constraining the goroutines we start to only the part of the slice we're passing in. Because of the lexical scope, we've made it impossible[1] to do the wrong thing, and so we don't need to synchronize memory access or share data through communication.

So what's the point? Why pursue confinement if we have synchronization available to us? The answer is improved performance and reduced cognitive load on developers. Synchronization comes with a cost, and if you can avoid it you won't have any critical sections, and therefore you won't have to pay the cost of synchronizing them. You also sidestep an entire class of issues possible with synchronization; developers simply

---

[1] I'm ignoring the possibility of manually manipulating memory via the unsafe package. It's called unsafe for a reason!

don't have to worry about these issues. Concurrent code that utilizes lexical confinement also has the benefit of usually being simpler to understand than concurrent code without lexically confined variables. This is because within the context of your lexical scope you can write synchronous code.

Having said that, it can be difficult to establish confinement, and so sometimes we have to fall back to our wonderful Go concurrency primitives.

The for-select Loop

Something you'll see over and over again in Go programs is the for-select loop. It's nothing more than something like this:

```
for { // Either loop infinitely or range over something
    select {
    // Do some work with channels
    }
}
```

There are a couple of different scenarios where you'll see this pattern pop up.

Sending iteration variables out on a channel
    Oftentimes you'll want to convert something that can be iterated over into values on a channel. This is nothing fancy, and usually looks something like this:

```
for _, s := range []string{"a", "b", "c"} {
    select {
    case <-done:
        return
    case stringStream <- s:
    }
}
```

Looping infinitely waiting to be stopped
    It's very common to create goroutines that loop infinitely until they're stopped. There are a couple variations of this one. Which one you choose is purely a stylistic preference.

The first variation keeps the **select** statement as short as possible:

```
for {
    select {
    case <-done:
        return
    default:
    }

    // Do non-preemptable work
}
```

If the done channel isn't closed, we'll exit the select statement and continue on to the rest of our for loop's body.

The second variation embeds the work in a default clause of the select statement:

```
for {
    select {
    case <-done:
        return
    default:
        // Do non-preemptable work
    }
}
```

When we enter the select statement, if the done channel hasn't been closed, we'll execute the default clause instead.

There's nothing more to this pattern, but it shows up all over the place, and so it's worth mentioning.

Preventing Goroutine Leaks

As we covered in the section "Goroutines" on page 37, we know goroutines are cheap and easy to create; it's one of the things that makes Go such a productive language. The runtime handles multiplexing the goroutines onto any number of operating system threads so that we don't often have to worry about that level of abstraction. But they *do* cost resources, and goroutines are not garbage collected by the runtime, so regardless of how small their memory footprint is, we don't want to leave them lying about our process. So how do we go about ensuring they're cleaned up?

Let's start from the beginning and think about this step by step: why would a goroutine exist? In Chapter 2, we established that goroutines represent units of work that may or may not run in parallel with each other. The goroutine has a few paths to termination:

- When it has completed its work.
- When it cannot continue its work due to an unrecoverable error.
- When it's told to stop working.

We get the first two paths for free—these paths are your algorithm—but what about work cancellation? This turns out to be the most important bit because of the network effect: if you've begun a goroutine, it's most likely cooperating with several other goroutines in some sort of organized fashion. We could even represent this interconnectedness as a graph: whether or not a child goroutine should continue executing might be predicated on knowledge of the state of many *other* goroutines. The parent goroutine (often the main goroutine) with this full contextual knowledge should be able to tell its child goroutines to terminate. We'll continue looking at large-scale goroutine interdependence in the next chapter, but for now let's consider how to ensure a single child goroutine is guaranteed to be cleaned up. Let's start with a simple example of a goroutine leak:

```
doWork := func(strings <-chan string) <-chan interface{} {
    completed := make(chan interface{})
    go func() {
        defer fmt.Println("doWork exited.")
        defer close(completed)
        for s := range strings {
            // Do something interesting
            fmt.Println(s)
        }
    }()
    return completed
}

doWork(nil)
// Perhaps more work is done here
fmt.Println("Done.")
```

Here we see that the main goroutine passes a nil channel into doWork. Therefore, the strings channel will never actually gets any strings written onto it, and the goroutine containing doWork will remain in memory for the lifetime of this process (we would even deadlock if we joined the goroutine within doWork and the main goroutine).

In this example, the lifetime of the process is very short, but in a real program, goroutines could easily be started at the beginning of a long-lived program. In the worst case, the main goroutine could *continue* to spin up goroutines throughout its life, causing creep in memory utilization.

The way to successfully mitigate this is to establish a signal between the parent goroutine and its children that allows the parent to signal cancellation to its children. By convention, this signal is usually a read-only channel named done. The parent goroutine passes this channel to the child goroutine and then closes the channel when it wants to cancel the child goroutine. Here's an example:

```
doWork := func(
    done <-chan interface{},
    strings <-chan string,
) <-chan interface{} { ❶
    terminated := make(chan interface{})
    go func() {
        defer fmt.Println("doWork exited.")
        defer close(terminated)
        for {
            select {
            case s := <-strings:
```

```
                    // Do something interesting
                    fmt.Println(s)
                case <-done: ❷
                    return
                }
            }
        }()
        return terminated
    }

    done := make(chan interface{})
    terminated := doWork(done, nil)

    go func() { ❸
        // Cancel the operation after 1 second.
        time.Sleep(1 * time.Second)
        fmt.Println("Canceling doWork goroutine...")
        close(done)
    }()

    <-terminated ❹
    fmt.Println("Done.")
```

❶ Here we pass the done channel to the doWork function. As a convention, this channel is the first parameter.

❷ On this line we see the ubiquitous for-select pattern in use. One of our case statements is checking whether our done channel has been signaled. If it has, we return from the goroutine.

❸ Here we create another goroutine that will cancel the goroutine spawned in doWork if more than one second passes.

❹ This is where we join the goroutine spawned from doWork with the main goroutine.

And the resulting output is:

```
Canceling doWork goroutine...
doWork exited.
Done.
```

You can see that despite passing in nil for our strings channel, our goroutine still exits successfully. Unlike the example before it, in this example we *do* join the two goroutines, and yet do not receive a deadlock. This is because before we join the two goroutines, we create a third goroutine to cancel the goroutine within doWork after a second. We have successfully eliminated our goroutine leak!

The previous example handles the case for goroutines receiving on a channel nicely, but what if we're dealing with the reverse situation: a goroutine blocked on attempting to write a value to a channel? Here's a quick example to demonstrate the issue:

```
newRandStream := func() <-chan int {
    randStream := make(chan int)
    go func() {
        defer fmt.Println("newRandStream closure exited.") ❶
        defer close(randStream)
        for {
            randStream <- rand.Int()
        }
    }()

    return randStream
}

randStream := newRandStream()
fmt.Println("3 random ints:")
for i := 1; i <= 3; i++ {
    fmt.Printf("%d: %d\n", i, <-randStream)
}
```

❶ Here we print out a message when the goroutine successfully terminates.

Running this code produces:

```
3 random ints:
1: 5577006791947779410
2: 8674665223082153551
3: 6129484611666145821
```

You can see from the output that the deferred fmt.Println statement never gets run. After the third iteration of our loop, our goroutine blocks trying to send the next random integer to a channel that is no longer being read from. We have no way of telling the producer it can stop. The solution, just like for the receiving case, is to provide the producer goroutine with a channel informing it to exit:

```
newRandStream := func(done <-chan interface{}) <-chan int {
    randStream := make(chan int)
    go func() {
        defer fmt.Println("newRandStream closure exited.")
        defer close(randStream)
        for {
            select {
            case randStream <- rand.Int():
            case <-done:
                return
            }
        }
    }()
```

```
        return randStream
    }

    done := make(chan interface{})
    randStream := newRandStream(done)
    fmt.Println("3 random ints:")
    for i := 1; i <= 3; i++ {
        fmt.Printf("%d: %d\n", i, <-randStream)
    }
    close(done)

    // Simulate ongoing work
    time.Sleep(1 * time.Second)
```

This code produces:

```
3 random ints:
1: 5577006791947779410
2: 8674665223082153551
3: 6129484611666145821
newRandStream closure exited.
```

We see now that the goroutine is being properly cleaned up.

Now that we know how to ensure goroutines don't leak, we can stipulate a convention: *If a goroutine is responsible for creating a goroutine, it is also responsible for ensuring it can stop the goroutine.*

This convention will help ensure your programs are composable and scale as they grow. We'll revisit this technique and rule more in the sections "Pipelines" on page 100 and "The context Package" on page 131. How we ensure goroutines are able to be stopped can differ depending on the type and purpose of goroutine, but they all build on the foundation of passing in a done channel.

The or-channel

At times you may find yourself wanting to combine one or more done channels into a single done channel that closes if any of its component channels close. It is perfectly acceptable, albeit verbose, to write a select statement that performs this coupling; however, sometimes you can't know the number of done channels you're working with at runtime. In this case, or if you just prefer a one-liner, you can combine these channels together using the *or-channel* pattern.

This pattern creates a composite done channel through recursion and goroutines. Let's have a look:

```
var or func(channels ...<-chan interface{}) <-chan interface{}
or = func(channels ...<-chan interface{}) <-chan interface{} { ❶
    switch len(channels) {
    case 0: ❷
```

```
        return nil
    case 1: ❸
        return channels[0]
    }

    orDone := make(chan interface{})
    go func() { ❹
        defer close(orDone)

        switch len(channels) {
        case 2: ❺
            select {
            case <-channels[0]:
            case <-channels[1]:
            }
        default: ❻
            select {
            case <-channels[0]:
            case <-channels[1]:
            case <-channels[2]:
            case <-or(append(channels[3:], orDone)...): ❻
            }
        }
    }()
    return orDone
}
```

❶ Here we have our function, or, which takes in a variadic slice of channels and returns a single channel.

❷ Since this is a recursive function, we must set up termination criteria. The first is that if the variadic slice is empty, we simply return a nil channel. This is consistant with the idea of passing in no channels; we wouldn't expect a composite channel to do anything.

❸ Our second termination criteria states that if our variadic slice only contains one element, we just return that element.

❹ Here is the main body of the function, and where the recursion happens. We create a goroutine so that we can wait for messages on our channels without blocking.

❺ Because of how we're recursing, every recursive call to or will at least have two channels. As an optimization to keep the number of goroutines constrained, we place a special case here for calls to or with only two channels.

❻ Here we recursively create an or-channel from all the channels in our slice after the third index, and then select from this. This recurrence relation will destruc-

ture the rest of the slice into or-channels to form a tree from which the first signal will return. We also pass in the orDone channel so that when goroutines up
the tree exit, goroutines down the tree also exit.

This is a fairly concise function that enables you to combine any number of channels
together into a single channel that will close as soon as any of its component channels
are closed, or written to. Let's take a look at how we can use this function. Here's a
brief example that takes channels that close after a set duration, and uses the or function to combine these into a single channel that closes:

```go
sig := func(after time.Duration) <-chan interface{}{ ❶
    c := make(chan interface{})
    go func() {
        defer close(c)
        time.Sleep(after)
    }()
    return c
}

start := time.Now() ❷
<-or(
    sig(2*time.Hour),
    sig(5*time.Minute),
    sig(1*time.Second),
    sig(1*time.Hour),
    sig(1*time.Minute),
)
fmt.Printf("done after %v", time.Since(start)) ❸
```

❶ This function simply creates a channel that will close when the time specified in
    the after elapses.

❷ Here we keep track of roughly when the channel from the or function begins to
    block.

❸ And here we print the time it took for the read to occur.

If you run this program you will get:

```
done after 1.000216772s
```

Notice that despite placing several channels in our call to or that take various times to
close, our channel that closes after one second causes the entire channel created by
the call to or to close. This is because—despite its place in the tree the or function
builds—it will always close first and thus the channels that depend on its closure will
close as well.

We achieve this terseness at the cost of additional goroutines—$f(x)=\lfloor x/2 \rfloor$ where x is
the number of goroutines—but remember that one of Go's strengths is the ability to

quickly create, schedule, and run goroutines, and the language actively encourages using goroutines to model problems correctly. Worrying about the number of goroutines created here is probably a premature optimization. Further, if at compile time you don't know how many done channels you're working with, there isn't any other way to combine done channels.

This pattern is useful to employ at the intersection of modules in your system. At these intersections, you tend to have multiple conditions for canceling trees of goroutines through your call stack. Using the or function, you can simply combine these together and pass it down the stack. We'll take a look at another way of doing this in "The context Package" on page 131 that is also very nice, and perhaps a bit more descriptive.

We'll also look at how we can use a variation of this pattern to form a more complicated pattern in "Replicated Requests" on page 172.

Error Handling

In concurrent programs, error handling can be difficult to get right. Sometimes, we spend so much time thinking about how our various processes will be sharing information and coordinating, we forget to consider how they'll gracefully handle errored states. When Go eschewed the popular exception model of errors, it made a statement that error handling was important, and that as we develop our programs, we should give our error paths the same attention we give our algorithms. In that spirit, let's take a look at how we do that when working with multiple concurrent processes.

The most fundamental question when thinking about error handling is, "Who should be responsible for handling the error?" At some point, the program needs to stop ferrying the error up the stack and actually do something with it. What is responsible for this?

With concurrent processes, this question becomes a little more complex. Because a concurrent process is operating independently of its parent or siblings, it can be difficult for it to reason about what the right thing to do with the error is. Take a look at the following code for an example of this issue:

```go
checkStatus := func(
    done <-chan interface{},
    urls ...string,
) <-chan *http.Response {
    responses := make(chan *http.Response)
    go func() {
        defer close(responses)
        for _, url := range urls {
            resp, err := http.Get(url)
            if err != nil {
                fmt.Println(err) ❶
```

```
            continue
        }
        select {
        case <-done:
            return
        case responses <- resp:
        }
    }
}()
    return responses
}

done := make(chan interface{})
defer close(done)

urls := []string{"https://www.google.com", "https://badhost"}
for response := range checkStatus(done, urls...) {
    fmt.Printf("Response: %v\n", response.Status)
}
```

❶ Here we see the goroutine doing its best to signal that there's an error. What else
can it do? It can't pass it back! How many errors is too many? Does it continue
making requests?

Running this code produces:

```
Response: 200 OK
Get https://badhost: dial tcp: lookup badhost on 127.0.1.1:53: no such host
```

Here we see that the goroutine has been given no choice in the matter. It can't simply
swallow the error, and so it does the only sensible thing: it prints the error and hopes
something is paying attention. Don't put your goroutines in this awkward position. I
suggest you separate your concerns: in general, your concurrent processes should
send their errors to another part of your program that has complete information
about the state of your program, and can make a more informed decision about what
to do. The following example demonstrates a correct solution to this problem:

```
type Result struct {  ❶
    Error error
    Response *http.Response
}
checkStatus := func(done <-chan interface{}, urls ...string) <-chan Result {  ❷
    results := make(chan Result)
    go func() {
        defer close(results)

        for _, url := range urls {
            var result Result
            resp, err := http.Get(url)
            result = Result{Error: err, Response: resp}  ❸
            select {
```

```
            case <-done:
                return
            case results <- result: ❹
            }
        }
    }()
    return results
}

done := make(chan interface{})
defer close(done)

urls := []string{"https://www.google.com", "https://badhost"}
for result := range checkStatus(done, urls...) {
    if result.Error != nil { ❺
        fmt.Printf("error: %v", result.Error)
        continue
    }
    fmt.Printf("Response: %v\n", result.Response.Status)
}
```

❶ Here we create a type that encompasses both the *http.Response and the error possible from an iteration of the loop within our goroutine.

❷ This line returns a channel that can be read from to retrieve results of an iteration of our loop.

❸ Here we create a Result instance with the Error and Response fields set.

❹ This is where we write the Result to our channel.

❺ Here, in our main goroutine, we are able to deal with errors coming out of the goroutine started by checkStatus intelligently, and with the full context of the larger program.

This code produces:

```
Response: 200 OK
error: Get https://badhost: dial tcp: lookup badhost on 127.0.1.1:53:
no such host
```

The key thing to note here is how we've coupled the potential result with the potential error. This represents the complete set of possible outcomes created from the goroutine checkStatus, and allows our main goroutine to make decisions about what to do when errors occur. In broader terms, we've successfully separated the concerns of error handling from our producer goroutine. This is desirable because the goroutine that spawned the producer goroutine—in this case our main goroutine—has more context about the running program, and can make more intelligent decisions about what to do with errors.

In the previous example, we simply wrote errors out to stdio, but we could do something else. Let's alter our program slightly so that it stops trying to check for status if three or more errors occur:

```
done := make(chan interface{})
defer close(done)

errCount := 0
urls := []string{"a", "https://www.google.com", "b", "c", "d"}
for result := range checkStatus(done, urls...) {
    if result.Error != nil {
        fmt.Printf("error: %v\n", result.Error)
        errCount++
        if errCount >= 3 {
            fmt.Println("Too many errors, breaking!")
            break
        }
        continue
    }
    fmt.Printf("Response: %v\n", result.Response.Status)
}
```

This code produces this output:

```
error: Get a: unsupported protocol scheme ""
Response: 200 OK
error: Get b: unsupported protocol scheme ""
error: Get c: unsupported protocol scheme ""
Too many errors, breaking!
```

You can see that because errors are returned from checkStatus and not handled internally within the goroutine, error handling follows the familiar Go pattern. This is a simple example, but it's not hard to imagine situations where the main goroutine is coordinating results from multiple goroutines and building up more complex rules for continuing or canceling child goroutines. Again, the main takeaway here is that errors should be considered first-class citizens when constructing values to return from goroutines. If your goroutine can produce errors, those errors should be tightly coupled with your result type, and passed along through the same lines of communication—just like regular synchronous functions.

Pipelines

When you write a program, you probably don't sit down and write one long function —at least I hope you don't! You construct abstractions in the form of functions, structs, methods, etc. Why do we do this? Partly to abstract away details that don't matter to the greater flow, and partly so that we can work on one area of code without affecting other areas. Have you ever had to make a change to a system and found yourself having to touch multiple areas just to make one logical change? It might be because that system suffers from poor abstraction.

A *pipeline* is just another tool you can use to form an abstraction in your system. In particular, it is a very powerful tool to use when your program needs to process streams, or batches of data. The word pipeline is believed to have first been used in 1856, and likely referred to a line of pipes that transported liquid from one place to another. We borrow this term in computer science because we're also transporting something from one place to another: data. A pipeline is nothing more than a series of things that take data in, perform an operation on it, and pass the data back out. We call each of these operations a *stage* of the pipeline.

By using a pipeline, you separate the concerns of each stage, which provides numerous benefits. You can modify stages independent of one another, you can mix and match how stages are combined independent of modifying the stages, you can process each stage concurrent to upstream or downstream stages, and you can *fan-out*, or *rate-limit* portions of your pipeline. We'll cover fan-out in the section "Fan-Out, Fan-In" on page 114, and we'll cover rate-limiting in Chapter 5. You don't have to worry about what these terms mean right now; let's start simple and just try and construct a pipeline stage.

As mentioned previously, a stage is just something that takes data in, performs a transformation on it, and sends the data back out. Here is a function that could be considered a pipeline stage:

```
multiply := func(values []int, multiplier int) []int {
    multipliedValues := make([]int, len(values))
    for i, v := range values {
        multipliedValues[i] = v * multiplier
    }
    return multipliedValues
}
```

This function takes a slice of integers in with a multiplier, loops through them multiplying as it goes, and returns a new transformed slice out. Looks like a boring function, right? Let's create another stage:

```
add := func(values []int, additive int) []int {
    addedValues := make([]int, len(values))
    for i, v := range values {
        addedValues[i] = v + additive
    }
    return addedValues
}
```

Another boring function! This one just creates a new slice and adds a value to each element. At this point, you might be wondering what makes these two functions pipeline stages and not just functions. Let's try combining them:

```
ints := []int{1, 2, 3, 4}
for _, v := range add(multiply(ints, 2), 1) {
    fmt.Println(v)
}
```

This code produces:

```
3
5
7
9
```

Look at how we combine add and multiply within the range clause. These are functions just like the ones you work with every day, but because we constructed them to have the properties of a pipeline stage, we're able to combine them to form a pipeline. That's interesting; what *are* the properties of a pipeline stage?

- A stage consumes and returns the same type.
- A stage must be reified[2] by the language so that it may be passed around. Functions in Go are reified and fit this purpose nicely.

Those of you familiar with functional programming may be nodding your head and thinking of terms like *higher order functions* and *monads*. Indeed, pipeline stages are very closely related to functional programming and can be considered a subset of monads. I won't go into monads or functional programming explicitly here, but they are interesting topics in their own right, and working knowledge of both topics is useful, although unnecessary, to draw on when trying to understand pipelines.

Here, our add and multiply stages satisfy all the properties of a pipeline stage: they both consume a slice of int and return a slice of int, and because Go has reified functions, we can pass add and multiple around. These properties give rise to the interesting properties of pipeline stages we mentioned earlier: namely it becomes very easy to combine our stages at a higher level without modifying the stages themselves.

For example, if we wanted to now add an additional stage to our pipeline to multiply by two, we'd simply wrap our previous pipeline in a new multiply stage, like so:

```
ints := []int{1, 2, 3, 4}
for _, v := range multiply(add(multiply(ints, 2), 1), 2) {
    fmt.Println(v)
}
```

---

2 Within the context of languages, reification means that the language exposes a concept to the developers so that they can work with it directly. Functions in Go are said to be reified because you can define variables that have a type of a function signature. This also means you can pass functions around your program.

Running this code produces:

```
6
10
14
18
```

Notice how we were able to do this without writing a new function, modifying any of the existing ones, or modifying what we do with the result of our pipeline. Maybe you're beginning to see the benefits of using the pipeline pattern. Of course we could write this code procedurally as well:

```
ints := []int{1, 2, 3, 4}
for _, v := range ints {
    fmt.Println(2*(v*2+1))
}
```

Initially, this looks much simpler, but as you'll see as we go along, the procedural code doesn't provide the same benefits a pipeline does when dealing with streams of data.

Notice how each stage is taking a slice of data and returning a slice of data? These stages are performing what we call *batch processing*. This just means that they operate on chunks of data all at once instead of one discrete value at a time. There is another type of pipeline stage that performs *stream processing*. This means that the stage receives and emits one element at a time.

There are pros and cons to batch processing versus stream processing, which we'll discuss in just a bit. For now, notice that for the original data to remain unaltered, each stage has to make a new slice of equal length to store the results of its calculations. That means that the memory footprint of our program at any one time is double the size of the slice we send into the start of our pipeline. Let's convert our stages to be stream oriented and see what that looks like:

```
multiply := func(value, multiplier int) int {
    return value * multiplier
}

add := func(value, additive int) int {
    return value + additive
}

ints := []int{1, 2, 3, 4}
for _, v := range ints {
    fmt.Println(multiply(add(multiply(v, 2), 1), 2))
}
```

This code produces:

```
6
10
14
18
```

Each stage is receiving and emitting a discrete value, and the memory footprint of our program is back down to only the size of the pipeline's input. But we had to pull the pipeline down into the body of the for loop and let the range do the heavy lifting of feeding our pipeline. Not only does this limit the reuse of how we feed the pipeline, but as we'll see later in this section, it also limits our ability to scale. We have other problems too. Effectively, we're instantiating our pipeline for every iteration of the loop. Though it's cheap to make function calls, we're making three function calls for each iteration of the loop. And what about concurrency? I stated earlier that one of the benefits of utilizing pipelines was the ability to process individual stages concurrently, and I mentioned something about *fan-out*. Where does all that come in?

I could probably extend our multiply and add functions a little more to introduce these concepts, but they've done their job of introducing the concept of a pipeline. It's time to begin learning what best practices exist for constructing pipelines in Go, and it begins with Go's *channel* primitive.

Best Practices for Constructing Pipelines

Channels are uniquely suited to constructing pipelines in Go because they fulfill all of our basic requirements. They can receive and emit values, they can safely be used concurrently, they can be ranged over, and they are reified by the language. Let's take a moment and convert the previous example to utilize channels instead:

```
generator := func(done <-chan interface{}, integers ...int) <-chan int {
    intStream := make(chan int)
    go func() {
        defer close(intStream)
        for _, i := range integers {
            select {
            case <-done:
                return
            case intStream <- i:
            }
        }
    }()
    return intStream
}

multiply := func(
  done <-chan interface{},
  intStream <-chan int,
  multiplier int,
) <-chan int {
    multipliedStream := make(chan int)
    go func() {
        defer close(multipliedStream)
        for i := range intStream {
            select {
            case <-done:
```

```
                    return
            case multipliedStream <- i*multiplier:
                }
            }
        }()
        return multipliedStream
    }

    add := func(
      done <-chan interface{},
      intStream <-chan int,
      additive int,
    ) <-chan int {
        addedStream := make(chan int)
        go func() {
            defer close(addedStream)
            for i := range intStream {
                select {
                case <-done:
                    return
                case addedStream <- i+additive:
                }
            }
        }()
        return addedStream
    }

    done := make(chan interface{})
    defer close(done)

    intStream := generator(done, 1, 2, 3, 4)
    pipeline := multiply(done, add(done, multiply(done, intStream, 2), 1), 2)

    for v := range pipeline {
        fmt.Println(v)
    }
```

This code produces:

```
6
10
14
18
```

It looks like we've replicated the desired output, but at the cost of having a lot more code. What exactly have we gained? First, let's examine what we've written. We now have three functions instead of two. They all look like they start one goroutine inside their bodies, and use the pattern we established in "Preventing Goroutine Leaks" on page 90 of taking in a channel to signal that the goroutine should exit. They all look like they return channels, and some of them look like they take in an additional channel as well. Interesting! Let's start breaking this down further:

```
done := make(chan interface{})
defer close(done)
```

The first thing our program does is create a done channel and call close on it in a
defer statement. As discussed previously, this ensures our program exits cleanly and
never leaks goroutines. Nothing new there. Next, let's take a look at the function,
generator:

```
generator := func(done <-chan interface{}, integers ...int) <-chan int {
    intStream := make(chan int)
    go func() {
        defer close(intStream)
        for _, i := range integers {
            select {
            case <-done:
                return
            case intStream <- i:
            }
        }
    }()
    return intStream
}

// ...

intStream := generator(done, 1, 2, 3, 4)
```

The generator function takes in a variadic slice of integers, constructs a buffered
channel of integers with a length equal to the incoming integer slice, starts a goroutine, and returns the constructed channel. Then, on the goroutine that was created,
generator ranges over the variadic slice that was passed in and sends the slices' values on the channel it created.

Note that the send on the channel shares a select statement with a selection on the
done channel. Again, this is the pattern we established in "Preventing Goroutine
Leaks" on page 90 to guard against leaking goroutines.

So in a nutshell, the generator function converts a discrete set of values into a stream
of data on a channel. Aptly, this type of function is called a *generator*. You'll see this
frequently when working with pipelines because at the beginning of the pipeline,
you'll always have some batch of data that you need to convert to a channel. We'll go
over a few examples of some fun generators in just a bit, but let's finish our analysis of
this program first. Next, we construct our pipeline:

```
pipeline := multiply(done, add(done, multiply(done, intStream, 2), 1), 2)
```

It's the same pipeline we've been working with all along: for a stream of numbers,
we'll multiply them by two, add one, and then multiply the result by two. This pipeline is similar to our pipeline utilizing functions in the previous example, but it is different in very important ways.

First, we're using channels. This is obvious but significant because it allows two things: at the end of our pipeline, we can use a range statement to extract the values, and at each stage we can safely execute concurrently because our inputs and outputs are safe in concurrent contexts.

Which brings us to our second difference: each stage of the pipeline is executing concurrently. This means that any stage only need wait for its inputs, and to be able to send its outputs. This turns out to have massive ramifications as we'll discover in the section "Fan-Out, Fan-In" on page 114, but for now we can simply note that it allows our stages to execute independent of one another for some slice of time.

Finally, in our example, we range over this pipeline and values are pulled through the system:

```
for v := range pipeline {
    fmt.Println(v)
}
```

Here is a table demonstrating how each of the values in the system will enter each channel, and when the channels will be closed. Iteration is the base-zero count of what iteration of the for loop we're on, and the value for each column is the value as it comes into the pipeline stage:

Iteration	Generator	Multiply	Add	Multiply	Value
0	1				
0		1			
0	2		2		
0		2		3	
0	3		4		6
1		3		5	
1	4		6		10
2	(closed)	4		7	
2		(closed)	8		14
3			(closed)	9	
3				(closed)	18

Let's also examine more closely our use of the pattern to signal goroutines to exit. When we're dealing with multiple interdependent goroutines, how does this pattern end up working? What would happen if we called close on the done channel before the program was finished executing?

To answer these questions, let's take a look at our pipeline construction one more time:

```
pipeline := multiply(done, add(done, multiply(done, intStream, 2), 1), 2)
```

The stages are interconnected in two ways: by the common done channel, and by the channels that are passed into subsequent stages of the pipeline. In other words, the channel created by the multiply function is passed into the add function, and so forth. Let's revisit the preceding table and, before allowing it to complete, call close on the done channel and see what happens:

Iteration	Generator	Multiply	Add	Multiply	Value
0	1				
0		1			
0	2		2		
0		2		3	
1	3		4		6
close(done)	(closed)	3		5	
		(closed)	6		
			(closed)	7	
				(closed)	
					(exit range)

See how closing the done channel cascades through the pipeline? This is made possible by two things in each stage of the pipeline:

- Ranging over the incoming channel. When the incoming channel is closed, the range will exit.

- The send sharing a select statement with the done channel.

Regardless of what state the pipeline stage is in—waiting on the incoming channel, or waiting on the send—closing the done channel will force the pipeline stage to terminate.

There is a recurrence relation at play here. At the beginning of the pipeline, we've established that we must convert discrete values into a channel. There are two points in this process that *must* be preemptable:

- Creation of the discrete value that is not nearly instantaneous.

- Sending of the discrete value on its channel.

The first is up to you. In our example, in the generator function, the discrete values are generated by ranging over the variadic slice, which is instantaneous enough that it doesn't need to be preemptable. The second is handled via our select statement and done channel, which ensures that generator is preemptable even if it is blocked attempting to write to intStream.

On the other end of the pipeline, the final stage is ensured preemptability by induction. It is preemptable because the channel we're ranging over will be closed when preempted, and therefore our range will break when this occurs. The final stage is preemptable because the stream we rely on is preemptable.

In between the beginning of the pipeline and the end of the pipeline, the code is always ranging over a channel and sending on another channel within a select statement containing a done channel.

If a stage is blocked on retrieving a value from the incoming channel, it will become unblocked when that channel is closed. We know by induction that the channel will be closed because it is either a stage written like the stage we are within, or the beginning of the pipeline that we have established is preemptable. If a stage is blocked on sending a value, it is preemptable thanks to the select statement.

Thus, our entire pipeline is always preemptable by closing the done channel. Cool, right?

Some Handy Generators

I promised earlier I would talk about some fun generators that might be widely useful. As a reminder, a generator for a pipeline is any function that converts a set of discrete values into a stream of values on a channel. Let's take a look at a generator called repeat:

```
repeat := func(
    done <-chan interface{},
    values ...interface{},
) <-chan interface{} {
    valueStream := make(chan interface{})
    go func() {
        defer close(valueStream)
        for {
            for _, v := range values {
                select {
                case <-done:
                    return
                case valueStream <- v:
                }
            }
        }
    }()
    return valueStream
}
```

This function will repeat the values you pass to it infinitely until you tell it to stop. Let's take a look at another generic pipeline stage that is helpful when used in combination with repeat, take:

```
    take := func(
        done <-chan interface{},
        valueStream <-chan interface{},
        num int,
    ) <-chan interface{} {
        takeStream := make(chan interface{})
        go func() {
            defer close(takeStream)
            for i := 0; i < num; i++ {
                select {
                case <-done:
                    return
                case takeStream <- <- valueStream:
                }
            }
        }()
        return takeStream
    }
```

This pipeline stage will only take the first num items off of its incoming valueStream and then exit. Together, the two can be very powerful:

```
    done := make(chan interface{})
    defer close(done)

    for num := range take(done, repeat(done, 1), 10) {
        fmt.Printf("%v ", num)
    }
```

Running this code produces:

```
    1 1 1 1 1 1 1 1 1 1
```

In this basic example, we create a repeat generator to generate an infinite number of ones, but then only take the first 10. Because the repeat generator's send blocks on the take stage's receive, the repeat generator is very efficient. Although we have the capability of generating an infinite stream of ones, we only generate N+1 instances where N is the number we pass into the take stage.

We can expand on this. Let's create another repeating generator, but this time, let's create one that repeatedly calls a function. Let's call it repeatFn:

```
    repeatFn := func(
        done <-chan interface{},
        fn func() interface{},
    ) <-chan interface{} {
        valueStream := make(chan interface{})
        go func() {
            defer close(valueStream)
            for {
                select {
                case <-done:
```

```
            return
        case valueStream <- fn():
        }
    }
}()
    return valueStream
}
```

Let's use it to generate 10 random numbers:

```
done := make(chan interface{})
defer close(done)

rand := func() interface{} { return rand.Int()}

for num := range take(done, repeatFn(done, rand), 10) {
    fmt.Println(num)
}
```

This produces:

```
5577006791947779410
8674665223082153551
6129484611666145821
4037200794235010051
3916589616287113937
6334824724549167320
605394647632969758
1443635317331776148
894385949183117216
2775422040480279449
```

That's pretty cool—an infinite channel of random integers generated on an as-needed basis!

You may be wondering why all of these generators and stages are receiving and sending on channels of interface{}. We could have just as easily written these functions to be specific to a type, or maybe written a Go generator.

Empty interfaces are a bit taboo in Go, but for pipeline stages it is my opinion that it's OK to deal in channels of interface{} so that you can use a standard library of pipeline patterns. As we discussed earlier, a lot of a pipeline's utility comes from reusable stages. This is best achieved when the stages operate at the level of specificity appropriate to itself. In the repeat and repeatFn generators, the concern is generating a stream of data by looping over a list or operator. With the take stage, the concern is limiting our pipeline. None of these operations require information about the types they're working on, but instead only require knowledge of the arity of their parameters.

When you need to deal in specific types, you can place a stage that performs the type assertion for you. The performance overhead of having an extra pipeline stage (and thus goroutine) and the type assertion are negligible, as we'll see in just a bit. Here's a small example that introduces a toString pipeline stage:

```
toString := func(
    done <-chan interface{},
    valueStream <-chan interface{},
) <-chan string {
    stringStream := make(chan string)
    go func() {
        defer close(stringStream)
        for v := range valueStream {
            select {
            case <-done:
                return
            case stringStream <- v.(string):
            }
        }
    }()
    return stringStream
}
```

And an example of how to use it:

```
done := make(chan interface{})
defer close(done)

var message string
for token := range toString(done, take(done, repeat(done, "I", "am."), 5)) {
    message += token
}

fmt.Printf("message: %s...", message)
```

This code produces:

```
message: Iam.Iam.I...
```

So let's prove to ourselves that the performance cost of genericizing portions of our pipeline is negligible. We'll write two benchmarking functions: one to test the generic stages, and one to test the type-specific stages:

```
func BenchmarkGeneric(b *testing.B) {
    done := make(chan interface{})
    defer close(done)

    b.ResetTimer()
    for range toString(done, take(done, repeat(done, "a"), b.N)) {
    }
}

func BenchmarkTyped(b *testing.B) {
    repeat := func(done <-chan interface{}, values ...string) <-chan string {
        valueStream := make(chan string)
        go func() {
```

```
            defer close(valueStream)
            for {
                for _, v := range values {
                    select {
                    case <-done:
                        return
                    case valueStream <- v:
                    }
                }
            }
        }()
        return valueStream
    }

    take := func(
        done <-chan interface{},
        valueStream <-chan string,
        num int,
    ) <-chan string {
        takeStream := make(chan string)
        go func() {
            defer close(takeStream)
            for i := num; i > 0 || i == -1; {
                if i != -1 {
                    i--
                }
                select {
                case <-done:
                    return
                case takeStream <- <-valueStream:
                }
            }
        }()
        return takeStream
    }

    done := make(chan interface{})
    defer close(done)

    b.ResetTimer()
    for range take(done, repeat(done, "a"), b.N) {
    }
}
```

And the results from running this code are:

BenchmarkGeneric-4	1000000	2266	ns/op
BenchmarkTyped-4	1000000	1181	ns/op
PASS			
ok	command-line-arguments	3.486s	

You can see that the type-specific stages are twice as fast, but only marginally faster in magnitude. Generally, the limiting factor on your pipeline will either be your generator, or one of the stages that is computationally intensive. If the generator isn't creating a stream from memory as with the `repeat` and `repeatFn` generators, you'll probably be I/O bound. Reading from disk or the network will likely eclipse the meager performance overhead shown here.

If one of your stages is computationally expensive, this will *certainly* eclipse this performance overhead. If this technique still leaves a bad taste in your mouth, you can always write a Go generator for creating your generator stages. Speaking of one stage being computationally expensive, how can we help mitigate this? Won't it rate-limit the entire pipeline?

For ways to help mitigate this, let's discuss the fan-out, fan-in technique.

Fan-Out, Fan-In

So you've got a pipeline set up. Data is flowing through your system beautifully, transforming as it makes its way through the stages you've chained together. It's like a beautiful stream; a beautiful, slow stream, and oh my god why is this taking so long?

Sometimes, stages in your pipeline can be particularly computationally expensive. When this happens, upstream stages in your pipeline can become blocked while waiting for your expensive stages to complete. Not only that, but the pipeline itself can take a long time to execute as a whole. How can we address this?

One of the interesting properties of pipelines is the ability they give you to operate on the stream of data using a combination of separate, often reorderable stages. You can even reuse stages of the pipeline multiple times. Wouldn't it be interesting to reuse a single stage of our pipeline on multiple goroutines in an attempt to parallelize pulls from an upstream stage? Maybe that would help improve the performance of the pipeline.

In fact, it turns out it can, and this pattern has a name: *fan-out, fan-in*.

Fan-out is a term to describe the process of starting multiple goroutines to handle input from the pipeline, and fan-in is a term to describe the process of combining multiple results into one channel.

So what makes a stage of a pipeline suited for utilizing this pattern? You might consider fanning out one of your stages if both of the following apply:

- It doesn't rely on values that the stage had calculated before.
- It takes a long time to run.

The property of order-independence is important because you have no guarantee in what order concurrent copies of your stage will run, nor in what order they will return.

Let's take a look at an example. In the following example, I've constructed a very inefficient way to find primes. We'll use a lot of the stages we created in "Pipelines" on page 100:

```
rand := func() interface{} { return rand.Intn(50000000) }

done := make(chan interface{})
defer close(done)

start := time.Now()

randIntStream := toInt(done, repeatFn(done, rand))
fmt.Println("Primes:")
for prime := range take(done, primeFinder(done, randIntStream), 10) {
    fmt.Printf("\t%d\n", prime)
}

fmt.Printf("Search took: %v", time.Since(start))
```

Here are the results of running this code:

```
Primes:
    24941317
    36122539
    6410693
    10128161
    25511527
    2107939
    14004383
    7190363
    45931967
    2393161
Search took: 23.437511647s
```

We're generating a stream of random numbers, capped at 50,000,000, converting the stream into an integer stream, and then passing that into our primeFinder stage. primeFinder naively begins to attempt to divide the number provided on the input stream by every number below it. If it's unsuccessful, it passes the value on to the next stage. Certainly, this is a horrible way to try and find prime numbers, but it fulfills our requirement of taking a *long* time.

In our for loop, we range over the found primes, print them out as they come in, and —thanks to our take stage—close the pipeline after 10 primes are found. We then print out how long the search took, and the done channel is closed by a defer statement and the pipeline is torn down.

To avoid duplicates in our results, we could introduce another stage in our pipeline to cache the primes that have been found in a set, but for simplicity, we'll just ignore these.

You can see it took roughly 23 seconds to find 10 primes. Not great. Normally we'd first look at the algorithm itself, maybe grab an algorithm cookbook, and see if we could improve things in each stage. But as the purpose of the stage here is to be slow, we'll instead look at how we can *fan-out* one or more of the stages to chew through slow operations more quickly.

This is a relatively simple example, so we only have two stages: random number generation and prime sieving. In a larger program, your pipeline might be composed of many more stages; how do we know which one to fan out? Remember our criteria from earlier: order-independence and duration. Our random integer generator is certainly order-independent, but it doesn't take a particularly long time to run. The primeFinder stage is also order-independent—numbers are either prime or not—and because of our naive algorithm, it certainly takes a long time to run. It looks like a good candidate for fanning out.

Fortunately the process of fanning out a stage in a pipeline is extraordinarily easy. All we have to do is start multiple versions of that stage. So instead of this:

```
primeStream := primeFinder(done, randIntStream)
```

We can do something like this:

```
numFinders := runtime.NumCPU()
finders := make([]<-chan int, numFinders)
for i := 0; i < numFinders; i++ {
    finders[i] = primeFinder(done, randIntStream)
}
```

Here we're starting up as many copies of this stage as we have CPUs. On my computer, runtime.NumCPU() returns eight, so I'll continue to use this number in our discussion. In production, we would probably do a little empirical testing to determine the optimal number of CPUs, but here we'll stay simple and assume that a CPU will be kept busy by only one copy of the findPrimes stage.

And that's it! We now have eight goroutines pulling from the random number generator and attempting to determine whether the number is prime. Generating random numbers shouldn't take much time, and so each goroutine for the findPrimes stage should be able to determine whether its number is prime and then have another random number available to it immediately.

We still have a problem though: now that we have four goroutines, we also have four channels, but our range over primes is only expecting one channel. This brings us to the *fan-in* portion of the pattern.

As we discussed earlier, fanning in means *multiplexing* or joining together multiple streams of data into a single stream. The algorithm to do so is relatively simple:

```
fanIn := func(
    done <-chan interface{},
    channels ...<-chan interface{},
) <-chan interface{} { ❶
    var wg sync.WaitGroup ❷
    multiplexedStream := make(chan interface{})

    multiplex := func(c <-chan interface{}) { ❸
        defer wg.Done()
        for i := range c {
            select {
            case <-done:
                return
            case multiplexedStream <- i:
            }
        }
    }

    // Select from all the channels
    wg.Add(len(channels)) ❹
    for _, c := range channels {
        go multiplex(c)
    }

    // Wait for all the reads to complete
    go func() { ❺
        wg.Wait()
        close(multiplexedStream)
    }()

    return multiplexedStream
}
```

❶ Here we take in our standard done channel to allow our goroutines to be torn down, and then a variadic slice of interface{} channels to fan-in.

❷ On this line we create a sync.WaitGroup so that we can wait until all channels have been drained.

❸ Here we create a function, multiplex, which, when passed a channel, will read from the channel, and pass the value read onto the multiplexedStream channel.

❹ This line increments the sync.WaitGroup by the number of channels we're multiplexing.

❺ Here we create a goroutine to wait for all the channels we're multiplexing to be drained so that we can close the `multiplexedStream` channel.

In a nutshell, fanning in involves creating the multiplexed channel consumers will read from, and then spinning up one goroutine for each incoming channel, and one goroutine to close the multiplexed channel when the incoming channels have all been closed. Since we're going to be creating a goroutine that is waiting on N other goroutines to complete, it makes sense to create a `sync.WaitGroup` to coordinate things. The `multiplex` function also notifies the `WaitGroup` that it's done.

An Additional Reminder

A naive implementation of the fan-in, fan-out algorithm only works if the order in which results arrive is unimportant. We have done nothing to guarantee that the order in which items are read from the `randIntStream` is preserved as it makes its way through the sieve. Later, we'll look at an example of a way to maintain order.

Let's put all of this together and see if we get any decrease in runtime:

```
done := make(chan interface{})
defer close(done)

start := time.Now()

rand := func() interface{} { return rand.Intn(50000000) }

randIntStream := toInt(done, repeatFn(done, rand))

numFinders := runtime.NumCPU()
fmt.Printf("Spinning up %d prime finders.\n", numFinders)
finders := make([]<-chan interface{}, numFinders)
fmt.Println("Primes:")
for i := 0; i < numFinders; i++ {
    finders[i] = primeFinder(done, randIntStream)
}

for prime := range take(done, fanIn(done, finders...), 10) {
    fmt.Printf("\t%d\n", prime)
}

fmt.Printf("Search took: %v", time.Since(start))
```

Here are the results:

```
Spinning up 8 prime finders.
Primes:
    6410693
    24941317
```

```
        10128161
        36122539
        25511527
        2107939
        14004383
        7190363
        2393161
        45931967
Search took: 5.438491216s
```

So down from ~23 seconds to ~5 seconds, not bad! This clearly demonstrates the
benefit of the fan-out, fan-in pattern, and it reiterates the utility of pipelines. We cut
our execution time by ~78% without drastically altering the structure of our program.

The or-done-channel

At times you will be working with channels from disparate parts of your system.
Unlike with pipelines, you can't make any assertions about how a channel will behave
when code you're working with is canceled via its done channel. That is to say, you
don't know if the fact that your goroutine was canceled means the channel you're
reading from will have been canceled. For this reason, as we laid out in "Preventing
Goroutine Leaks" on page 90, we need to wrap our read from the channel with a
select statement that also selects from a done channel. This is perfectly fine, but
doing so takes code that's easily read like this:

```
for val := range myChan {
    // Do something with val
}
```

And explodes it out into this:

```
loop:
for {
    select {
    case <-done:
        break loop
    case maybeVal, ok := <-myChan:
        if ok == false {
            return // or maybe break from for
        }
        // Do something with val
    }
}
```

This can get busy quite quickly—especially if you have nested loops. Continuing with
the theme of utilizing goroutines to write clearer concurrent code, and not prematurely optimizing, we can fix this with a single goroutine. We encapsulate the verbo-
sity so that others don't have to:

```
orDone := func(done, c <-chan interface{}) <-chan interface{} {
    valStream := make(chan interface{})
    go func() {
        defer close(valStream)
        for {
            select {
            case <-done:
                return
            case v, ok := <-c:
                if ok == false {
                    return
                }
                select {
                case valStream <- v:
                case <-done:
                }
            }
        }
    }()
    return valStream
}
```

Doing this allows us to get back to simple for loops, like so:

```
for val := range orDone(done, myChan) {
    // Do something with val
}
```

You may find edge cases in your code where you need a tight loop utilizing a series of select statements, but I would encourage you to try for readability first, and avoid premature optimization.

The tee-channel

Sometimes you may want to split values coming in from a channel so that you can send them off into two separate areas of your codebase. Imagine a channel of user commands: you might want to take in a stream of user commands on a channel, send them to something that executes them, and also send them to something that logs the commands for later auditing.

Taking its name from the tee command in Unix-like systems, the *tee-channel* does just this. You can pass it a channel to read from, and it will return two separate channels that will get the same value:

```
tee := func(
    done <-chan interface{},
    in <-chan interface{},
) (_, _ <-chan interface{}) { <-chan interface{}) {
    out1 := make(chan interface{})
    out2 := make(chan interface{})
    go func() {
```

```
        defer close(out1)
        defer close(out2)
        for val := range orDone(done, in) {
            var out1, out2 = out1, out2 ❶
            for i := 0; i < 2; i++ { ❷
                select {
                case <-done:
                case out1<-val:
                    out1 = nil ❸
                case out2<-val:
                    out2 = nil ❸
                }
            }
        }
    }()
    return out1, out2
}
```

❶ We will want to use local versions of out1 and out2, so we shadow these variables.

❷ We're going to use one select statement so that writes to out1 and out2 don't block each other. To ensure both are written to, we'll perform two iterations of the select statement: one for each outbound channel.

❸ Once we've written to a channel, we set its shadowed copy to nil so that further writes will block and the other channel may continue.

Notice that writes to out1 and out2 are tightly coupled. The iteration over in cannot continue until both out1 and out2 have been written to. Usually this is not a problem as handling the throughput of the process reading from each channel should be a concern of something other than the tee command anyway, but it's worth noting. Here's a quick example to demonstrate:

```
done := make(chan interface{})
defer close(done)

out1, out2 := tee(done, take(done, repeat(done, 1, 2), 4))

for val1 := range out1 {
    fmt.Printf("out1: %v, out2: %v\n", val1, <-out2)
}
```

Utilizing this pattern, it's easy to continue using channels as the join points of your system.

The bridge-channel

In some circumstances, you may find yourself wanting to consume values from a sequence of channels:

```
<-chan <-chan interface{}
```

This is slightly different than coalescing a slice of channels into a single channel, as we saw in "The or-channel" on page 94 or "Fan-Out, Fan-In" on page 114. A sequence of channels suggests an ordered write, albeit from different sources. One example might be a pipeline stage whose lifetime is intermittent. If we follow the patterns we established in "Confinement" on page 85 and ensure channels are owned by the goroutines that write to them, every time a pipeline stage is restarted within a new goroutine, a new channel would be created. This means we'd effectively have a sequence of channels. We'll explore this scenario more in "Healing Unhealthy Goroutines" on page 188.

As a consumer, the code may not care about the fact that its values come from a sequence of channels. In that case, dealing with a channel of channels can be cumbersome. If we instead define a function that can destructure the channel of channels into a simple channel—a technique called *bridging* the channels—this will make it much easier for the consumer to focus on the problem at hand. Here's how we can achieve that:

```
bridge := func(
    done <-chan interface{},
    chanStream <-chan <-chan interface{},
) <-chan interface{} {
    valStream := make(chan interface{}) ❶
    go func() {
        defer close(valStream)
        for { ❷
            var stream <-chan interface{}
            select {
            case maybeStream, ok := <-chanStream:
                if ok == false {
                    return
                }
                stream = maybeStream
            case <-done:
                return
            }
            for val := range orDone(done, stream) { ❸
                select {
                case valStream <- val:
                case <-done:
                }
            }
        }
    }
```

```
        }()
        return valStream
    }
```

❶ This is the channel that will return all values from `bridge`.

❷ This loop is responsible for pulling channels off of `chanStream` and providing them to a nested loop for use.

❸ This loop is responsible for reading values off the channel it has been given and repeating those values onto `valStream`. When the stream we're currently looping over is closed, we break out of the loop performing the reads from this channel, and continue with the next iteration of the loop, selecting channels to read from. This provides us with an unbroken stream of values.

This is pretty straightforward code. Now we can use `bridge` to help present a single-channel facade over a channel of channels. Here's an example that creates a series of 10 channels, each with one element written to them, and passes these channels into the `bridge` function:

```
genVals := func() <-chan <-chan interface{} {
    chanStream := make(chan (<-chan interface{}))
    go func() {
        defer close(chanStream)
        for i := 0; i < 10; i++ {
            stream := make(chan interface{}, 1)
            stream <- i
            close(stream)
            chanStream <- stream
        }
    }()
    return chanStream
}

for v := range bridge(nil, genVals()) {
    fmt.Printf("%v ", v)
}
```

Running this produces:

```
0 1 2 3 4 5 6 7 8 9
```

Thanks to `bridge`, we can use the channel of channels from within a single range statement and focus on our loop's logic. Destructuring the channel of channels is left to code that is specific to this concern.

Queuing

Sometimes it's useful to begin accepting work for your pipeline even though the pipeline is not yet ready for more. This process is called *queuing*.

All this means is that once your stage has completed some work, it stores it in a temporary location in memory so that other stages can retrieve it later, and your stage doesn't need to hold a reference to it. In the section on "Channels" on page 64, we discussed *buffered channels*, a type of queue, but we haven't really made much use of them since—and for good reason.

While introducing queuing into your system is very useful, it's usually one of the last techniques you want to employ when optimizing your program. Adding queuing prematurely can hide synchronization issues such as deadlocks and livelocks, and further, as your program converges toward correctness, you may find that you need more or less queuing.

So what is queuing good for? Let's begin to answer that question by addressing one of the common mistakes people make when trying to tune the performance of a system: introducing queues to try and address performance concerns. Queuing will almost never speed up the total runtime of your program; it will only allow the program to behave differently.

To understand why, let's take a look at a simple pipeline:

```
done := make(chan interface{})
defer close(done)

zeros := take(done, 3, repeat(done, 0))
short := sleep(done, 1*time.Second, zeros)
long := sleep(done, 4*time.Second, short)
pipeline := long
```

This pipeline chains together four stages:

1. A repeat stage that generates an endless stream of 0s.

2. A stage that cancels the previous stages after seeing three items.

3. A "short" stage that sleeps one second.

4. A "long" stage that sleeps four seconds.

For the purposes of this example, let's assume that stages 1 and 2 are instantaneous, and let's focus on how the stages that sleep affect the runtime of the pipeline.

Here's a table examining the time t, the iteration i, and how long the long and short stages have left to move to their next value.

Time(t)	i	Long stage	Short stage
0	0		1s
1	0	4s	1s
2	0	3s	(blocked)
3	0	2s	(blocked)
4	0	1s	(blocked)
5	1	4s	1s
6	1	3s	(blocked)
7	1	2s	(blocked)
8	1	1s	(blocked)
9	2	4s	(close)
10	2	3s	
11	2	2s	
12	2	1s	
13	3	(close)	

You can see that this pipeline takes roughly 13 seconds to run. The short stage takes about 9 seconds to complete.

What happens if we modify the pipeline to include a buffer? Let's examine the same pipeline with a buffer of 2 introduced between the long and short stages:

```
done := make(chan interface{})
defer close(done)

zeros := take(done, 3, repeat(done, 0))
short := sleep(done, 1*time.Second, zeros)
buffer := buffer(done, 2, short)    // Buffers sends from short by 2
long := sleep(done, 4*time.Second, short)
pipeline := long
```

Here's the runtime:

Time(t)	i	Long stage	Buffer	Short stage
0	0		0/2	1s
1	0	4s	0/2	1s
2	0	3s	1/2	1s
3	0	2s	2/2	(close)
4	0	1s	2/2	
5	1	4s	1/2	
6	1	3s	1/2	
7	1	2s	1/2	
8	1	1s	1/2	

Time(t)	i	Long stage	Buffer	Short stage
9	2	4s	0/2	
10	2	3s	0/2	
11	2	2s	0/2	
12	2	1s	0/2	
13	3	(close)		

The entire pipeline still took 13 seconds! But look at the short stage's runtime. It's complete after only 3 seconds as opposed to the 9 seconds it took previously. We've cut this stage's runtime by two thirds! But if the entire pipeline still takes 13 seconds to execute, how does this help us?

Picture instead the following pipeline:

```
p := processRequest(done, acceptConnection(done, httpHandler))
```

Here the pipeline doesn't exit until it's canceled, and the stage that is accepting connections doesn't stop accepting connections until the pipeline is canceled. In this scenario, you wouldn't want connections to your program to begin timing out because your processRequest stage was blocking your acceptConnection stage. You want your acceptConnection stage to be unblocked as much as possible. Otherwise the users of your program might begin seeing their requests denied altogether.

So the answer to our question of the utility of introducing a queue isn't that the runtime of one of stages has been reduced, but rather that the time it's in a *blocking state* is reduced. This allows the stage to continue doing its job. In this example, users would likely experience lag in their requests, but they wouldn't be denied service altogether.

In this way, the true utility of queues is to *decouple stages* so that the runtime of one stage has no impact on the runtime of another. Decoupling stages in this manner then cascades to alter the runtime behavior of the system as a whole, which can be either good or bad depending on your system.

We then come to the question of tuning your queuing. Where should the queues be placed? What should the buffer size be? The answers to these questions depend on the nature of your pipeline.

Let's begin by analyzing situations in which queuing *can* increase the overall performance of your system. The only applicable situations are:

- If batching requests in a stage saves time.
- If delays in a stage produce a feedback loop into the system.

One example of the first situation is a stage that buffers input in something faster (e.g., memory) than it is designed to send to (e.g., disk). This is, of course, the entire purpose of Go's bufio package. Here's an example that demonstrates a simple comparison of a buffered write to a queue versus an unbuffered write:

```
func BenchmarkUnbufferedWrite(b *testing.B) {
    performWrite(b, tmpFileOrFatal())
}

func BenchmarkBufferedWrite(b *testing.B) {
    bufferredFile := bufio.NewWriter(tmpFileOrFatal())
    performWrite(b, bufio.NewWriter(bufferredFile))
}

func tmpFileOrFatal() *os.File {
    file, err := ioutil.TempFile("", "tmp")
    if err != nil {
        log.Fatal("error: %v", err)
    }
    return file
}

func performWrite(b *testing.B, writer io.Writer) {
    done := make(chan interface{})
    defer close(done)

    b.ResetTimer()
    for bt := range take(done, repeat(done, byte(0)), b.N) {
        writer.Write([]byte{bt.(byte)})
    }
}
```

```
go test -bench=. src/concurrency-patterns-in-go/queuing/buffering_test.go
```

And here are the results of running this benchmark:

BenchmarkUnbufferedWrite-8	500000	3969	ns/op
BenchmarkBufferedWrite-8	1000000	1356	ns/op
PASS			
ok	command-line-arguments	3.398s	

As anticipated, the buffered write is faster than the unbuffered write. This is because in `bufio.Writer`, the writes are *queued* internally into a buffer until a sufficient chunk has been accumulated, and then the chunk is written out. This process is often called *chunking*, for obvious reasons.

Chunking is faster because `bytes.Buffer` must grow its allocated memory to accommodate the bytes it must store. For various reasons, growing memory is expensive; therefore, the less times we have to grow, the more efficient our system as a whole will perform. Thus, queuing has increased the performance of our system as a whole.

This is only a simple in-memory example of chunking, but you may encounter chunking frequently in the field. Usually anytime performing an operation requires an overhead, chunking may increase system performance. Some examples of this are opening database transactions, calculating message checksums, and allocating contiguous space.

Aside from chunking, queuing can also help if your algorithm can be optimized by supporting lookbehinds, or ordering.

The second scenario, where a delay in a stage causes more input into the pipeline, is a little more difficult to spot, but also more important because it can lead to a systemic collapse of your upstream systems.

This idea is often referred to as a *negative feedback loop*, downward-spiral, or even death-spiral. This is because a recurrent relation exists between the pipeline and its upstream systems; the rate at which upstream stages or systems submit new requests is somehow linked to how efficient the pipeline is.

If the efficiency of the pipeline drops below a certain critical threshold, the systems upstream from the pipeline begin increasing their inputs into the pipeline, which causes the pipeline to lose more efficiency, and the death-spiral begins. Without some sort of fail-safe, the system utilizing the pipeline will never recover.

By introducing a queue at the entrance to the pipeline, you can break the feedback loop at the cost of creating lag for requests. From the perspective of the caller into the pipeline, the request appears to be processing, but taking a very long time. As long as the caller doesn't time out, your pipeline will remain stable. If the caller does time out, you need to be sure you support some kind of check for readiness when dequeuing. If you don't, you can inadvertently create a feedback loop by processing dead requests thereby decreasing the efficiency of your pipeline.

Have You Ever Witnessed a Death-Spiral?

If you've ever attempted to access some hot new system when it first came online (e.g., new game servers, websites for product launches, etc.), and the site kept bouncing despite the developer's best efforts, congratulations! You've likely witnessed a negative feedback loop.

Invariably the development team tries different things until someone realizes they need a queue, and one is hastily implemented.

Then the customers begin complaining about queue times!

So from our examples we can begin to see a pattern emerge; queuing should be implemented either:

- At the entrance to your pipeline.
- In stages where batching will lead to higher efficiency.

You may be tempted to add queuing elsewhere—e.g., after a computationally expensive stage—but avoid that temptation! As we've learned, there are only a few situations where queuing will decrease the runtime of your pipeline, and peppering in queuing in an attempt to work around this can have disastrous consequences.

This is not intuitive at first; to understand why, we have to discuss throughput of the pipeline. Don't worry, it's not that difficult, and it will also help us answer the question of how to determine how large our queues should be.

In queuing theory, there is a law that—with enough sampling—predicts the throughput of your pipeline. It's called *Little's Law*, and you only need to know a few things to understand and make use of it.

Let's first define Little's Law algebraicly. It is commonly expressed as: $L = \lambda W$, where:

- L = the average number of units in the system.
- λ = the average arrival rate of units.
- W = the average time a unit spends in the system.

This equation only applies to so-called *stable* systems. In a pipeline, a stable system is one in which the rate that work enters the pipeline, or *ingress*, is equal to the rate in which it exits the system, or *egress*. If the rate of ingress exceeds the rate of egress, your system is *unstable* and has entered a *death-spiral*. If the rate of ingress is less than the rate of egress, you still have an unstable system, but all that's happening is that your resources aren't being utilized completely. Not the worst situation in the world, but maybe you care about this if the underutilization is found on a vast scale (e.g., clusters or data centers).

So let's assume that our pipeline is stable. If we want to decrease W, the average time a unit spends in the system by a factor of n, we only have one option: to decrease the average number of units in the system: $L/n = \lambda * W/n$. And we can only decrease the average number of units in the system if we increase the rate of egress. Also notice that if we add queues to our stages, we're increasing L, which either increases the arrival rate of units ($nL = n\lambda * W$) or increases the average time a unit spends in the system ($nL = \lambda * nW$). Through Little's Law, we have proven that queuing will not help decrease the amount of time spent in a system.

Also notice that since we're observing our pipeline as a whole, reducing W by a factor of n is distributed throughout all stages of our pipeline. In our case, Little's Law should really be defined like this:

$$L = \lambda \Sigma_i W_i$$

That's another way of saying that your pipeline will only be as fast as your slowest stage. Optimize indiscriminately!

So Little's Law is neat! This simple equation opens up all kinds of ways to analyze our pipeline. Let's use it to ask some interesting questions. During our analysis, let's assume our pipeline has three stages.

Let's try and determine how many requests per second our pipeline can handle. Let's assume we enable sampling on our pipeline and find that 1 request (r) takes about 1 second to make it through the pipeline. Let's plug in those numbers!

```
3r = λr/s * 1s
3r/s = λr/s
λr/s = 3r/s
```

We set L to 3 because each stage in our pipeline is processing a request. We then set W to 1 second, do a little algebra, and voilà! In this pipeline, we can handle three requests per second.

What about determining how large our queue needs to be to handle a desired number of requests. Can Little's Law help us answer that?

Let's say our sampling indicates that a request takes 1 ms to process. What size would our queue have to be to handle 100,000 requests per second? Again, let's plug in the numbers!

```
Lr-3r = 100,000r/s * 0.0001s
Lr-3r = 10r
Lr = 7r
```

Again, our pipeline has three stages, so we'll decrement L by 3. We set λ to 100,000 r/s, and find that if we want to field that many requests, our queue should have a capacity of 7. Remember that as you increase the queue size, it takes your work longer to make it through the system! You're effectively trading system utilization for lag.

Something that Little's Law can't provide insight on is handling failure. Keep in mind that if for some reason your pipeline panics, you'll lose all the requests in your queue. This might be something to guard against if re-creating the requests is difficult or won't happen. To mitigate this, you can either stick to a queue size of zero, or you can move to a *persistent queue*, which is simply a queue that is persisted somewhere that can be later read from should the need arise.

Queuing can be useful in your system, but because of its complexity, it's usually one of the last optimizations I would suggest implementing.

The context Package

As we've seen, in concurrent programs it's often necessary to preempt operations because of timeouts, cancellation, or failure of another portion of the system. We've looked at the idiom of creating a done channel, which flows through your program and cancels all blocking concurrent operations. This works well, but it's also somewhat limited.

It would be useful if we could communicate extra information alongside the simple notification to cancel: why the cancellation was occuring, or whether or not our function has a deadline by which it needs to complete.

It turns out that the need to wrap a done channel with this information is very common in systems of any size, and so the Go authors decided to create a standard pattern for doing so. It started out as an experiment that lived outside the standard library, but in Go 1.7, the context package was brought into the standard library, making this a standard Go idiom to consider when working with concurrent code.

If we take a peek into the context package, we see that it's very simple:

```
var Canceled = errors.New("context canceled")
var DeadlineExceeded error = deadlineExceededError{}

type CancelFunc
type Context

func Background() Context
func TODO() Context
func WithCancel(parent Context) (ctx Context, cancel CancelFunc)
func WithDeadline(parent Context, deadline time.Time) (Context, CancelFunc)
func WithTimeout(parent Context, timeout time.Duration) (Context, CancelFunc)
func WithValue(parent Context, key, val interface{}) Context
```

We'll revisit these types and functions in a bit, but for now let's focus on the Context type. This is the type that will flow through your system much like a done channel does. If you use the context package, each function that is downstream from your top-level concurrent call would take in a Context as its first argument. The type looks like this:

```
type Context interface {

    // Deadline returns the time when work done on behalf of this
    // context should be canceled. Deadline returns ok==false when no
```

```
    // deadline is set. Successive calls to Deadline return the same
    // results.
    Deadline() (deadline time.Time, ok bool)

    // Done returns a channel that's closed when work done on behalf
    // of this context should be canceled. Done may return nil if this
    // context can never be canceled. Successive calls to Done return
    // the same value.
    Done() <-chan struct{}

    // Err returns a non-nil error value after Done is closed. Err
    // returns Canceled if the context was canceled or
    // DeadlineExceeded if the context's deadline passed. No other
    // values for Err are defined.  After Done is closed, successive
    // calls to Err return the same value.
    Err() error

    // Value returns the value associated with this context for key,
    // or nil if no value is associated with key. Successive calls to
    // Value with the same key returns the same result.
    Value(key interface{}) interface{}
}
```

This also looks pretty simple. There's a Done method which returns a channel that's closed when our function is to be preempted. There's also some new, but easy to understand methods: a Deadline function to indicate if a goroutine will be canceled after a certain time, and an Err method that will return non-nil if the goroutine was canceled. But the Value method looks a little out of place. What's it for?

The Go authors noticed that one of the primary uses of goroutines was programs that serviced requests. Usually in these programs, request-specific information needs to be passed along in addition to information about preemption. This is the purpose of the Value function. We'll talk about this more in a bit, but for now we just need to know that the context package serves two primary purposes:

- To provide an API for canceling branches of your call-graph.
- To provide a data-bag for transporting request-scoped data through your call-graph.

Let's focus on the first aspect: cancellation.

As we learned in "Preventing Goroutine Leaks" on page 90, cancellation in a function has three aspects:

- A goroutine's parent may want to cancel it.
- A goroutine may want to cancel its children.

- Any blocking operations within a goroutine need to be preemptable so that it may be canceled.

The context package helps manage all three of these.

As we mentioned, the Context type will be the first argument to your function. If you look at the methods on the Context interface, you'll see that there's nothing present that can mutate the state of the underlying structure. Further, there's nothing that allows the function accepting the Context to cancel it. This protects functions up the call stack from children canceling the context. Combined with the Done method, which provides a done channel, this allows the Context type to safely manage cancellation from its antecedents.

This raises a question: if a Context is immutable, how do we affect the behavior of cancellations in functions below a current function in the call stack?

This is where the functions in the context package become important. Let's take a look at a few of them one more time to refresh our memory:

```
func WithCancel(parent Context) (ctx Context, cancel CancelFunc)
func WithDeadline(parent Context, deadline time.Time) (Context, CancelFunc)
func WithTimeout(parent Context, timeout time.Duration) (Context, CancelFunc)
```

Notice that all these functions take in a Context and return one as well. Some of these also take in other arguments like deadline and timeout. The functions all generate new instances of a Context with the options relative to these functions.

WithCancel returns a new Context that closes its done channel when the returned cancel function is called. WithDeadline returns a new Context that closes its done channel when the machine's clock advances past the given deadline. WithTimeout returns a new Context that closes its done channel after the given timeout duration.

If your function needs to cancel functions below it in the call-graph in some manner, it will call one of these functions and pass in the Context it was given, and then pass the Context returned into its children. If your function doesn't need to modify the cancellation behavior, the function simply passes on the Context it was given.

In this way, successive layers of the call-graph can create a Context that adheres to their needs without affecting their parents. This provides a very composable, elegant solution for how to manage branches of your call-graph.

In this spirit, instances of a Context are meant to flow through your program's call-graph. In an object-oriented paradigm, it's common to store references to often-used data as member variables, but it's important to *not* do this with instances of context.Context. Instances of context.Context may look equivalent from the outside, but internally they may change at every stack-frame. For this reason, it's important to always pass instances of Context into your functions. This way functions have the Context intended for it, and not the Context intended for a stack-frame N levels up the stack.

At the top of your asynchronous call-graph, your code probably won't have been passed a Context. To start the chain, the context package provides you with two functions to create empty instances of Context:

```
func Background() Context
func TODO() Context
```

Background simply returns an empty Context. TODO is not meant for use in production, but also returns an empty Context; TODO's intended purpose is to serve as a placeholder for when you don't know which Context to utilize, or if you expect your code to be provided with a Context, but the upstream code hasn't yet furnished one.

So let's put all this to use. Let's look at an example that uses the done channel pattern, and see what benefits we might gain from switching to use of the context package. Here is a program that concurrently prints a greeting and a farewell:

```
func main() {
    var wg sync.WaitGroup
    done := make(chan interface{})
    defer close(done)

    wg.Add(1)
    go func() {
        defer wg.Done()
        if err := printGreeting(done); err != nil {
            fmt.Printf("%v", err)
            return
        }
    }()

    wg.Add(1)
    go func() {
        defer wg.Done()
        if err := printFarewell(done); err != nil {
            fmt.Printf("%v", err)
            return
        }
    }()

    wg.Wait()
}

func printGreeting(done <-chan interface{}) error {
    greeting, err := genGreeting(done)
    if err != nil {
        return err
    }
    fmt.Printf("%s world!\n", greeting)
```

```
        return nil
    }

    func printFarewell(done <-chan interface{}) error {
        farewell, err := genFarewell(done)
        if err != nil {
            return err
        }
        fmt.Printf("%s world!\n", farewell)
        return nil
    }

    func genGreeting(done <-chan interface{}) (string, error) {
        switch locale, err := locale(done); {
        case err != nil:
            return "", err
        case locale == "EN/US":
            return "hello", nil
        }
        return "", fmt.Errorf("unsupported locale")
    }

    func genFarewell(done <-chan interface{}) (string, error) {
        switch locale, err := locale(done); {
        case err != nil:
            return "", err
        case locale == "EN/US":
            return "goodbye", nil
        }
        return "", fmt.Errorf("unsupported locale")
    }

    func locale(done <-chan interface{}) (string, error) {
        select {
        case <-done:
            return "", fmt.Errorf("canceled")
        case <-time.After(1*time.Minute):
        }
        return "EN/US", nil
    }
```

Running this code produces:

```
goodbye world!
hello world!
```

Ignoring the race condition (we could receive our farewell before we're greeted!), we can see that we have two branches of our program running concurrently. We've set up the standard preemption method by creating a done channel and passing it down through our call-graph. If we close the done channel at any point in main, both branches will be canceled.

By introducing goroutines in main, we've opened up the possibility of controlling this program in a few different and interesting ways. Maybe we want genGreeting to time out if it takes too long. Maybe we don't want genFarewell to invoke locale if we know its parent is going to be canceled soon. At each stack-frame, a function can affect the entirety of the call stack below it.

Using the done channel pattern, we could accomplish this by wrapping the incoming done channel in other done channels and then returning if any of them fire, but we wouldn't have the extra information about deadlines and errors a Context gives us.

To make comparing the done channel pattern to the use of the context package easier, let's represent this program as a tree. Each node in the tree represents an invocation of a function.

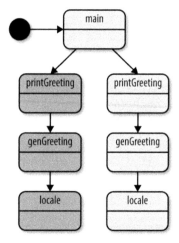

Let's modify our program to use the context package instead of a done channel. Because we now have the flexibility of a context.Context, we can introduce a fun scenario.

Let's say that genGreeting only wants to wait one second before abandoning the call to locale—a timeout of one second. We also want to build some smart logic into main. If printGreeting is unsuccessful, we also want to cancel our call to printFare well. After all, it wouldn't make sense to say goodbye if we don't say hello!

Implementing this with the context package is trivial:

```go
func main() {
    var wg sync.WaitGroup
    ctx, cancel := context.WithCancel(context.Background()) ❶
    defer cancel()
```

```go
    wg.Add(1)
    go func() {
        defer wg.Done()

        if err := printGreeting(ctx); err != nil {
            fmt.Printf("cannot print greeting: %v\n", err)
            cancel() ❷
        }
    }()

    wg.Add(1)
    go func() {
        defer wg.Done()
        if err := printFarewell(ctx); err != nil {
            fmt.Printf("cannot print farewell: %v\n", err)
        }
    }()

    wg.Wait()
}

func printGreeting(ctx context.Context) error {
    greeting, err := genGreeting(ctx)
    if err != nil {
        return err
    }
    fmt.Printf("%s world!\n", greeting)
    return nil
}

func printFarewell(ctx context.Context) error {
    farewell, err := genFarewell(ctx)
    if err != nil {
        return err
    }
    fmt.Printf("%s world!\n", farewell)
    return nil
}

func genGreeting(ctx context.Context) (string, error) {
    ctx, cancel := context.WithTimeout(ctx, 1*time.Second) ❸
    defer cancel()

    switch locale, err := locale(ctx); {
    case err != nil:
        return "", err
    case locale == "EN/US":
        return "hello", nil
    }
    return "", fmt.Errorf("unsupported locale")
}
```

```
func genFarewell(ctx context.Context) (string, error) {
    switch locale, err := locale(ctx); {
    case err != nil:
        return "", err
    case locale == "EN/US":
        return "goodbye", nil
    }
    return "", fmt.Errorf("unsupported locale")
}

func locale(ctx context.Context) (string, error) {
    select {
    case <-ctx.Done():
        return "", ctx.Err() ❹
    case <-time.After(1 * time.Minute):
    }
    return "EN/US", nil
}
```

❶ Here main creates a new Context with context.Background() and wraps it with context.WithCancel to allow for cancellations.

❷ On this line, main will cancel the Context if there is an error returned from print Greeting.

❸ Here genGreeting wraps its Context with context.WithTimeout. This will automatically cancel the returned Context after 1 second, thereby canceling any children it passes the Context into, namely locale.

❹ This line returns the reason why the Context was canceled. This error will bubble all the way up to main, which will cause the cancellation at ❷.

Here are the results of running this code:

```
cannot print greeting: context deadline exceeded
cannot print farewell: context canceled
```

Let's use our call-graph to understand what's going on. The numbers here correspond to the code callouts in the preceding example.

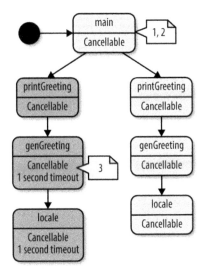

We can see from our output that the system works perfectly. Since we ensure `locale` takes at least one minute to run, our call in `genGreeting` will always time out, which means `main` will always cancel the call-graph below `printFarewell`.

Notice how `genGreeting` was able to build up a custom `context.Context` to meet its needs without having to affect its parent's `Context`. If `genGreeting` were to return successfully, and `printGreeting` needed to make another call, it could do so without leaking information about how `genGreeting` operated. This composability enables you to write large systems without mixing concerns throughout your call-graph.

We can make another improvement on this program: since we know `locale` takes roughly one minute to run, in `locale` we can check to see whether we were given a deadline, and if so, whether we'll meet it. This example demonstrates using the `context.Context`'s `Deadline` method to do so:

```go
func main() {
    var wg sync.WaitGroup
    ctx, cancel := context.WithCancel(context.Background())
    defer cancel()

    wg.Add(1)
    go func() {
        defer wg.Done()

        if err := printGreeting(ctx); err != nil {
            fmt.Printf("cannot print greeting: %v\n", err)
            cancel()
        }
    }()
```

```go
    wg.Add(1)
    go func() {
        defer wg.Done()
        if err := printFarewell(ctx); err != nil {
            fmt.Printf("cannot print farewell: %v\n", err)
        }
    }()

    wg.Wait()
}

func printGreeting(ctx context.Context) error {
    greeting, err := genGreeting(ctx)
    if err != nil {
        return err
    }
    fmt.Printf("%s world!\n", greeting)
    return nil
}

func printFarewell(ctx context.Context) error {
    farewell, err := genFarewell(ctx)
    if err != nil {
        return err
    }
    fmt.Printf("%s world!\n", farewell)
    return nil
}

func genGreeting(ctx context.Context) (string, error) {
    ctx, cancel := context.WithTimeout(ctx, 1*time.Second)
    defer cancel()

    switch locale, err := locale(ctx); {
    case err != nil:
        return "", err
    case locale == "EN/US":
        return "hello", nil
    }
    return "", fmt.Errorf("unsupported locale")
}

func genFarewell(ctx context.Context) (string, error) {
    switch locale, err := locale(ctx); {
    case err != nil:
        return "", err
    case locale == "EN/US":
        return "goodbye", nil
    }
    return "", fmt.Errorf("unsupported locale")
}
```

```
func locale(ctx context.Context) (string, error) {
    if deadline, ok := ctx.Deadline(); ok { ❶
        if deadline.Sub(time.Now().Add(1*time.Minute)) <= 0 {
            return "", context.DeadlineExceeded
        }
    }

    select {
    case <-ctx.Done():
        return "", ctx.Err()
    case <-time.After(1 * time.Minute):
    }
    return "EN/US", nil
}
```

❶ Here we check to see whether our Context has provided a deadline. If it did, and our system's clock has advanced past the deadline, we simply return with a special error defined in the context package, DeadlineExceeded.

Although the difference in this iteration of the program is small, it allows the locale function to fail fast. In programs that may have a high cost for calling the next bit of functionality, this may save a significant amount of time, but at the very least it also allows the function to fail immediately instead of having to wait for the actual time-out to occur. The only catch is that you have to have some idea of how long your subordinate call-graph will take—an exercise that can be very difficult.

This brings us to the other half of what the context package provides: a data-bag for a Context to store and retrieve request-scoped data. Remember that oftentimes when a function creates a goroutine and Context, it's starting a process that will service requests, and functions further down the stack may need information about the request. Here's an example of how to store data within the Context, and how to retrieve it:

```
func main() {
    ProcessRequest("jane", "abc123")
}

func ProcessRequest(userID, authToken string) {
    ctx := context.WithValue(context.Background(), "userID", userID)
    ctx = context.WithValue(ctx, "authToken", authToken)
    HandleResponse(ctx)
}

func HandleResponse(ctx context.Context) {
    fmt.Printf(
        "handling response for %v (%v)",
        ctx.Value("userID"),
        ctx.Value("authToken"),
```

```
    )
}
```

This produces:

```
handling response for jane (abc123)
```

Pretty simple stuff. The only qualifications are that:

- The key you use must satisfy Go's notion of *comparability*; that is, the equality operators == and != need to return correct results when used.
- Values returned must be safe to access from multiple goroutines.

Since both the Context's key and value are defined as interface{}, we lose Go's type-safety when attempting to retrieve values. The key could be a different type, or slightly different than the key we provide. The value could be a different type than we're expecting. For these reasons, the Go authors recommend you follow a few rules when storing and retrieving value from a Context.

First, they recommend you define a custom key-type in your package. As long as other packages do the same, this prevents collisions within the Context. As a reminder as to why, let's take a look at a short program that attempts to store keys in a map that have different types, but the same underlying value:

```
type foo int
type bar int

m := make(map[interface{}]int)
m[foo(1)] = 1
m[bar(1)] = 2

fmt.Printf("%v", m)
```

This produces:

```
map[1:1 1:2]
```

You can see that though the underlying values are the same, the different type information differentiates them within a map. Since the type you define for your package's keys is unexported, other packages cannot conflict with keys you generate within your package.

Since we don't export the keys we use to store the data, we must therefore export functions that retrieve the data for us. This works out nicely since it allows consumers of this data to use static, type-safe functions.

When you put all of this together, you get something like the following example:

```
func main() {
    ProcessRequest("jane", "abc123")
}
```

```
type ctxKey int

const (
    ctxUserID ctxKey = iota
    ctxAuthToken
)

func UserID(c context.Context) string {
    return c.Value(ctxUserID).(string)
}

func AuthToken(c context.Context) string {
    return c.Value(ctxAuthToken).(string)
}

func ProcessRequest(userID, authToken string) {
    ctx := context.WithValue(context.Background(), ctxUserID, userID)
    ctx = context.WithValue(ctx, ctxAuthToken, authToken)
    HandleResponse(ctx)
}

func HandleResponse(ctx context.Context) {
    fmt.Printf(
        "handling response for %v (auth: %v)",
        UserID(ctx),
        AuthToken(ctx),
    )
}
```

Running this code produces:

```
handling response for jane (auth: abc123)
```

We now have a type-safe way to retrieve values from the Context, and—if the consumers were in a different package—they wouldn't know or care what keys were used to store the information. However, this technique does pose a problem.

In the previous example, let's say HandleResponse *did* live in another package named response, and let's say the package ProcessRequest lived in a package named process. The process package would have to import the response package to make the call to HandleResponse, but HandleResponse would have no way to access the accessor functions defined in the process package because importing process would form a circular dependency. Because the types used to store the keys in Context are private to the process package, the response package has no way to retrieve this data!

This coerces the architecture into creating packages centered around data types that are imported from multiple locations. This certainly isn't a bad thing, but it's something to be aware of.

The context package is pretty neat, but it hasn't been uniformly lauded. Within the Go community, the context package has been somewhat controversial. The cancellation aspect of the package has been pretty well received, but the ability to store arbitrary data in a Context, and the type-unsafe manner in which the data is stored, have caused some divisiveness. Although we have partially abated the lack of type-safety with our accessor functions, we could still introduce bugs by storing incorrect types. However, the larger issue is definitely the nature of *what* developers should store in instances of Context.

The most prevalent guidance on what's appropriate is this somewhat ambiguous comment in the context package:

```
Use context values only for request-scoped data that transits processes and
API boundaries, not for passing optional parameters to functions.
```

It's pretty clear what an optional parameter is (you shouldn't be using a Context to fulfill your secret desire for Go to support optional parameters), but what is "request-scoped data"? Supposedly it "transits processes and API boundaries," but that could describe lots of things. The best way I've found to define it is to come up with some heuristics with your team, and evaluate them in code reviews. Here are my heuristics:

1) *The data should transit process or API boundaries.*
   If you generate the data in your process' memory, it's probably not a good candidate to be request-scoped data unless you also pass it across an API boundary.

2) *The data should be immutable.*
   If it's not, then by definition what you're storing did not come from the request.

3) *The data should trend toward simple types.*
   If request-scoped data is meant to transit process and API boundaries, it's much easier for the other side to pull this data out if it doesn't also have to import a complex graph of packages.

4) *The data should be data, not types with methods.*
   Operations are logic and belong on the things consuming this data.

5) *The data should help decorate operations, not drive them.*
   If your algorithm behaves differently based on what is or isn't included in its Context, you have likely crossed over into the territory of optional parameters.

These aren't hard-and-fast rules; they're heuristics. However, if you find data you're storing in a Context violating all five of these guidelines, you might want to take a long look at what you're choosing to do.

Another dimension to consider is how many layers this data might need to traverse before utilization. If there are a few frameworks and tens of functions between where the data is accepted and where it is used, do you want to lean toward verbose, self-documenting function signatures, and add the data as a parameter? Or would you rather place it in a Context and thereby create an invisible dependency? There are merits to each approach, and in the end it's a decision you and your team will have to make.

Even with these heuristics, whether or not a value is request-scoped data remains a difficult question to answer. Take a look at the following table. It lists my opinions on whether or not each type of data fulfills the five heuristics I've listed. Do you agree?

Data	1	2	3	4	5
Request ID	✓	✓	✓	✓	✓
User ID	✓	✓	✓	✓	
URL	✓	✓			
API Server Connection					
Authorization Token	✓	✓	✓	✓	
Request Token	✓	✓	✓		

Sometimes it's clear that something should not be stored in a context, as it is with API server connections, but sometimes it's not so clear. What about an authorization token? It's immutable, and it's likely a slice of bytes, but won't the receivers of this data use it to determine whether to field the request? Does this data belong in a context? To further muddy the waters, what is acceptable on one team may not be acceptable on another.

Ultimately there are no easy answers here. The package has been brought into the standard library, and so you must form *some* opinion on its use, but that opinion could (and probably should) change depending on what project you're touching. The final advice I'd leave you with is that the cancellation functionality provided by Context is very useful, and your feelings about the data-bag shouldn't deter you from using it.

Summary

We've covered a lot of ground in this chapter. We've combined Go's concurrency primitives to form patterns that help write maintainable concurrent code. Now that you're familiar with these patterns, we can discuss how we can incorporate these patterns into *other* patterns that will help you to write large systems. The next chapter will give you an overview of techniques for doing just that.

CHAPTER 5

Concurrency at Scale

Now that you've learned some common patterns for utilizing concurrency within Go, let's turn our attention to composing these patterns into a series of practices that will enable you to write large, composable systems that scale.

In this chapter, we'll discuss ways to scale concurrent operations within a single process, and also begin looking at how concurrency comes into play when dealing with more than one process.

Error Propagation

With concurrent code, and especially distributed systems, it's both easy for something to go wrong in your system, and difficult to understand why it happened. You can save yourself, your team, and your users a whole lot of pain by carefully considering how issues propagate through your system, and how they end up being represented to the user. In the section "Error Handling" on page 97, we discussed *how* to propagate errors from goroutines, but we didn't spend any time discussing what those errors should look like, or how errors should flow through a large and complex system. Let's spend some time here discussing a philosophy of error propagation. What follows is an opinionated framework for handling errors in concurrent systems.

Many developers make the mistake of thinking of error propagation as secondary, or "other," to the flow of their system. Careful consideration is given to how data flows through the system, but errors are something that are tolerated and ferried up the stack without much thought, and ultimately dumped in front of the user. Go attempted to correct this bad practice by forcing users to handle errors at every frame in the call stack, but it's still common to see errors treated as second-class citizens to the system's control flow. With just a little forethought, and minimal overhead, you can make your error handling an asset to your system, and a delight to your users.

First let's examine what errors are. When do they occur, and what benefit do they provide?

Errors indicate that your system has entered a state in which it cannot fulfill an operation that a user either explicitly or implicitly requested. Because of this, it needs to relay a few pieces of critical information:

What happened.
> This is the part of the error that contains information about what happened, e.g., "disk full," "socket closed," or "credentials expired." This information is likely to be generated implicitly by whatever it was that generated the errors, although you can probably decorate this with some context that will help the user.

When and where it occurred.
> Errors should always contain a complete stack trace starting with how the call was initiated and ending with where the error was instantiated. The stack trace should *not* be contained in the error message (more on this in a bit), but should be easily accessible when handling the error up the stack.

> Further, the error should contain information regarding the context it's running within. For example, in a distributed system, it should have some way of identifying what machine the error occurred on. Later, when trying to understand what happened in your system, this information will be invaluable.

> In addition, the error should contain the time on the machine the error was instantiated on, in UTC.

A friendly user-facing message.
> The message that gets displayed to the user should be customized to suit your system and its users. It should only contain abbreviated and relevant information from the previous two points. A friendly message is human-centric, gives some indication of whether the issue is transitory, and should be about one line of text.

How the user can get more information.
> At some point, someone will likely want to know, in detail, what happened when the error occurred. Errors that are presented to users should provide an ID that can be cross-referenced to a corresponding log that displays the full information of the error: time the error occurred (not the time the error was logged), the stack trace—everything you stuffed into the error when it was created. It can also be helpful to include a hash of the stack trace to aid in aggregating like issues in bug trackers.

By default, no error will contain all of this information without your intervention. Therefore, you could take the stance that any error that is propagated to the user *without* this information is a mistake, and therefore a bug. This leads to a general framework we can use to think about errors. It's possible to place all errors into one of two categories:

- Bugs
- Known edge cases (e.g., broken network connections, failed disk writes, etc.)

Bugs are errors that you have not customized to your system, or "raw" errors—your known edge cases. Sometimes this is intentional; you may be OK with letting errors from edge cases reach your users while you get the first few iterations of your system out the door. Sometimes this is by accident. But if you agree with the approach I've laid out, raw errors are always bugs. This distinction will prove useful when determining how to propagate errors, how your system grows over time, and what to ultimately display to the user.

Imagine a large system with multiple modules:

Let's say an error occurs in the "Low Level Component" and we've crafted a well-formed error there to be passed up the stack. Within the context of the "Low Level Component," this error might be considered well-formed, but within the context of our system, it may not be. Let's take the stance that at the boundaries of each component, all incoming errors must be wrapped in a well-formed error for the component our code is within. For example, if we were in "Intermediary Component," and we were calling code from "Low Level Component," which might error, we could have this:

```
func PostReport(id string) error {
    result, err := lowlevel.DoWork()
    if err != nil {
        if _, ok := err.(lowlevel.Error); ok { ❶
            err = WrapErr(err, "cannot post report with id %q", id) ❷
        }
        return err
    }
    // ...
}
```

❶ Here we check to ensure we're receiving a well-formed error. If we aren't, we'll simply ferry the malformed error up the stack to indicate a bug.

❷ Here we use a hypothetical function call to wrap the incoming error with pertinent information for our module, and to give it a new type. Note that wrapping the error might involve *hiding* some low-level details that may not be important for the user within this context.

The low-level details of where the root of the error occurred (e.g., what goroutine, machine, stack trace, etc.) are still filled in when the error is initially instantiated, but our architecture dictates that at module boundaries we convert the error to our module's error type—potentially filling in pertinent information. Now, any error that escapes *our* module without our module's error type can be considered malformed, and a bug. Note that it is only necessary to wrap errors in this fashion at your *own* module boundaries—public functions/methods—or when your code can add valuable context. Usually this prevents the need for wrapping errors in most of the code.

Taking this stance allows our system to grow very organically. We can be sure that incoming errors are well-formed, and we in turn can ensure we are giving thought to how errors escape our module. Error correctness becomes an emergent property of our system. We also concede perfection from the start by explicitly handling malformed errors, and by doing so we have given ourselves a framework to take mistakes and correct them over time. Malformed errors are clearly delineated both by type and, as we'll see, by what is presented to the user.

As we established, all errors should be logged with as much information as is available. But when displaying errors to users, this is where the distinction between bugs and known edge cases comes in.

When our user-facing code receives a well-formed error, we can be confident that at all levels in our code, care was taken to craft the error message, and we can simply log it and print it out for the user to see. The confidence that we get from seeing an error with the correct type cannot be understated.

When malformed errors, or bugs, are propagated up to the user, we should also log the error, but then display a friendly message to the user stating something unexpected has happened. If we support automatic error reporting in our system, the error should be reported back as a bug. If we don't, we might suggest the user file a bug report. Note that the malformed error might actually contain useful information, but we cannot guarantee this, and so—since the only guarantee we do have is that the error is not customized—we should bluntly display a human-centric message about what happened.

Remember that in either case, with well- or malformed errors, we will have included a log ID in the message to give the user something to refer back to should the user want more information. Thus, even if bugs were to contain useful information, the curious user still has means to investigate.

Let's take a look at a complete example. This example won't be extremely robust (e.g., the error type is perhaps simplistic), and the call stack is linear, which obfuscates the fact that it's only necessary to wrap errors at module boundaries. Also, it's difficult to represent functions in different packages in a book, and so we'll be pretending.

First, let's create an error type that can contain all of the aspects of a well-formed error we've discussed:

```go
type MyError struct {
    Inner      error
    Message    string
    StackTrace string
    Misc       map[string]interface{}
}

func wrapError(err error, messagef string, msgArgs ...interface{}) MyError {
    return MyError{
        Inner:      err, ❶
        Message:    fmt.Sprintf(messagef, msgArgs...),
        StackTrace: string(debug.Stack()), ❷
        Misc:       make(map[string]interface{}), ❸
    }
}

func (err MyError) Error() string {
    return err.Message
}
```

❶ Here we store the error we're wrapping. We always want to be able to get back to the lowest-level error in case we need to investigate what happened.

❷ This line of code takes note of the stack trace when the error was created. A more sophisticated error type might elide the stack-frame from wrapError.

❸ Here we create a catch-all for storing miscellaneous information. This is where we might store the concurrent ID, a hash of the stack trace, or other contextual information that might help in diagnosing the error.

Next, let's create a module, lowlevel:

```go
// "lowlevel" module

type LowLevelErr struct {
    error
}

func isGloballyExec(path string) (bool, error) {
    info, err := os.Stat(path)
    if err != nil {
        return false, LowLevelErr{(wrapError(err, err.Error()))} ❶
    }
    return info.Mode().Perm()&0100 == 0100, nil
}
```

➊ Here we wrap the raw error from calling `os.Stat` with a customized error. In this case we are OK with the message coming out of this error, and so we won't mask it.

Then, let's create another module, `intermediate`, which calls functions from the `low level` package:

```
// "intermediate" module

type IntermediateErr struct {
    error
}

func runJob(id string) error {
    const jobBinPath = "/bad/job/binary"
    isExecutable, err := isGloballyExec(jobBinPath)
    if err != nil {
        return err ➊
    } else if isExecutable == false {
        return wrapError(nil, "job binary is not executable")
    }

    return exec.Command(jobBinPath, "--id="+id).Run() ➊
}
```

➊ Here we are passing on errors from the `lowlevel` module. Because of our architectural decision to consider errors passed on from other modules without wrapping them in our own type bugs, this will cause us issues later.

Finally, let's create a top-level `main` function that calls functions from the `intermedi ate` package. This is the user-facing portion of our program:

```
func handleError(key int, err error, message string) {
    log.SetPrefix(fmt.Sprintf("[logID: %v]: ", key))
    log.Printf("%#v", err) ➌
    fmt.Printf("[%v] %v", key, message)
}

func main() {
    log.SetOutput(os.Stdout)
    log.SetFlags(log.Ltime|log.LUTC)

    err := runJob("1")
    if err != nil {
        msg := "There was an unexpected issue; please report this as a bug."
        if _, ok := err.(IntermediateErr); ok { ➊
            msg = err.Error()
        }
        handleError(1, err, msg) ➋
    }
}
```

❶ Here we check to see if the error is of the expected type. If it is, we know it's a well-crafted error, and we can simply pass its message on to the user.

❷ On this line we bind the log and error message together with an ID of 1. We could easily make this increase monotonically, or use a GUID to ensure a unique ID.

❸ Here we log out the full error in case someone needs to dig into what happened.

When we run this, we get a log message that contains:

```
[logID: 1]: 21:46:07 main.LowLevelErr{error:main.MyError{Inner:
(*os.PathError)(0xc4200123f0),
Message:"stat /bad/job/binary: no such file or directory",
StackTrace:"goroutine 1 [running]:
runtime/debug.Stack(0xc420012420, 0x2f, 0xc420045d80)
    /home/kate/.guix-profile/src/runtime/debug/stack.go:24 +0x79
main.wrapError(0x530200, 0xc4200123f0, 0xc420012420, 0x2f, 0x0, 0x0,
0x0, 0x0, 0x0, 0x0, ...)
    /tmp/babel-79540aE/go-src-7954NTK.go:22 +0x62
main.isGloballyExec(0x4d1313, 0xf, 0xc420045eb8, 0x487649, 0xc420056050)
    /tmp/babel-79540aE/go-src-7954NTK.go:37 +0xaa
main.runJob(0x4cfada, 0x1, 0x4d4c35, 0x22)
    /tmp/babel-79540aE/go-src-7954NTK.go:47 +0x48
main.main()
    /tmp/babel-79540aE/go-src-7954NTK.go:67 +0x63
", Misc:map[string]interface {}{}}}
```

And a message to stdout that contains:

```
[1] There was an unexpected issue; please report this as a bug.
```

We can see that somewhere along this error's path, it was not handled correctly, and because we cannot be sure the error message is fit for human consumption, we print a simple error out stating that something unexpected happened (true if we are following this methodology). If we look back up to our intermediate module, we recall why: we didn't wrap the errors from the lowlevel module. Let's correct that and see what happens:

```go
// "intermediate" module

type IntermediateErr struct {
    error
}

func runJob(id string) error {
    const jobBinPath = "/bad/job/binary"
    isExecutable, err := isGloballyExec(jobBinPath)
    if err != nil {
        return IntermediateErr{wrapError(
            err,
```

```
                "cannot run job %q: requisite binaries not available",
                id,
        )} ❶
    } else if isExecutable == false {
        return wrapError(
            nil,
            "cannot run job %q: requisite binaries are not executable",
            id,
        )
    }

    return exec.Command(jobBinPath, "--id="+id).Run()
}
```

❶ Here we are now customizing the error with a crafted message. In this case, we want to obfuscate the low-level details of why the job isn't running because we feel it's not important information to consumers of our module.

```
func handleError(key int, err error, message string) {
    log.SetPrefix(fmt.Sprintf("[logID: %v]: ", key))
    log.Printf("%#v", err)
    fmt.Printf("[%v] %v", key, message)
}

func main() {
    log.SetOutput(os.Stdout)
    log.SetFlags(log.Ltime|log.LUTC)

    err := runJob("1")
    if err != nil {
        msg := "There was an unexpected issue; please report this as a bug."
        if _, ok := err.(IntermediateErr); ok {
            msg = err.Error()
        }
        handleError(1, err, msg)
    }
}
```

Now when we run the updated code, we get a similar log message:

```
[logID: 1]: 22:11:04 main.IntermediateErr{error:main.MyError
{Inner:main.LowLevelErr{error:main.MyError{Inner:(*os.PathError)
(0xc4200123f0), Message:"stat /bad/job/binary: no such file or directory",
StackTrace:"goroutine 1 [running]:
runtime/debug.Stack(0xc420012420, 0x2f, 0x0)
    /home/kate/.guix-profile/src/runtime/debug/stack.go:24 +0x79
main.wrapError(0x530200, 0xc4200123f0, 0xc420012420, 0x2f, 0x0, 0x0,
0x0, 0x0, 0x0, 0x0, ...)
    /tmp/babel-79540aE/go-src-7954DTN.go:22 +0xbb
main.isGloballyExec(0x4d1313, 0xf, 0x4daecc, 0x30, 0x4c5800)
    /tmp/babel-79540aE/go-src-7954DTN.go:39 +0xc5
main.runJob(0x4cfada, 0x1, 0x4d4c19, 0x22)
    /tmp/babel-79540aE/go-src-7954DTN.go:51 +0x4b
```

```
main.main()
    /tmp/babel-79540aE/go-src-7954DTN.go:71 +0x63
", Misc:map[string]interface {}{}}}, Message:"cannot run job \"1\":
requisite binaries not available", StackTrace:"goroutine 1 [running]:
runtime/debug.Stack(0x4d63f0, 0x33, 0xc420045e40)
    /home/kate/.guix-profile/src/runtime/debug/stack.go:24 +0x79
main.wrapError(0x530380, 0xc42000a370, 0x4d63f0, 0x33,
0xc420045e40, 0x1, 0x1, 0x0, 0x0, 0x0, ...)
    /tmp/babel-79540aE/go-src-7954DTN.go:22 +0xbb
main.runJob(0x4cfada, 0x1, 0x4d4c19, 0x22)
    /tmp/babel-79540aE/go-src-7954DTN.go:53 +0x356
main.main()
    /tmp/babel-79540aE/go-src-7954DTN.go:71 +0x63
", Misc:map[string]interface {}{}}}
```

But our error message is now exactly what we want users to see:

```
[1] cannot run job "1": requisite binaries not available
```

There are error packages[1] that are compatible with this approach, but it will be up to you to implement this technique using whatever error package you decide to use. The good news is that this technique is organic; you can canvas your top-level error handling and delineate between bugs and well-crafted errors, and then progressively ensure that all the errors you create are considered well-crafted.

Timeouts and Cancellation

When working with concurrent code, timeouts and cancellations are going to turn up frequently. As we'll see in this section, among other things, timeouts are crucial to creating a system with behavior you can understand. Cancellation is one natural response to a timeout. We'll also explore other reasons a concurrent process might be canceled.

So what are the reasons we might want our concurrent processes to support timeouts? Here are a few:

System saturation
As we discussed in the section "Queuing" on page 124, if our system is saturated (i.e., if its ability to process requests is at capacity), we may want requests at the edges of our system to time out rather than take a long time to field them. Which path you take depends on your problem space, but here are some general guidelines for when to time out:

- If the request is unlikely to be repeated when it is timed out.

---

1 I recommend *http://github.com/pkg/errors*.

- If you don't have the resources to store the requests (e.g., memory for in-memory queues, disk space for persisted queues).

- If the need for the request, or the data it's sending, will go stale (we'll discuss this next). If a request is likely to be repeated, your system will develop an overhead from accepting and timing out requests. This can lead to a death-spiral if the overhead becomes greater than our system's capacity. However, this is a moot point if we lack the system resources required to store the request in a queue. And even if we meet these two guidelines, there is little point in enqueueing a request whose need will expire by the time we can process it. This brings us to our next reason to support timeouts.

Stale data

Sometimes data has a window within which it must be processed before more relevant data is available, or the need to process the data has expired. If a concurrent process takes longer to process the data than this window, we would want to time out and cancel the concurrent process. For instance, if our concurrent process is dequeing a request after a long wait, the request or its data might have become obsolete during the queuing process.

If this window is known beforehand, it would make sense to pass our concurrent process a `context.Context` created with `context.WithDeadline`, or `context.WithTimeout`. If the window is not known beforehand, we'd want the parent of the concurrent process to be able to cancel the concurrent process when the need for the request is no longer present. `context.WithCancel` is perfect for this purpose.

Attempting to prevent deadlocks

In a large system—especially distributed systems—it can sometimes be difficult to understand the way in which data might flow, or what edge cases might turn up. It is not unreasonable, and even recommended, to place timeouts on *all* of your concurrent operations to guarantee your system won't deadlock. The timeout period doesn't have to be close to the actual time it takes to perform your concurrent operation. The timeout period's purpose is only to prevent deadlock, and so it only needs to be short enough that a deadlocked system will unblock in a reasonable amount of time for your use case.

Remember from the section "Deadlocks, Livelocks, and Starvation" on page 10 that attempting to avoid a deadlock by setting a timeout can potentially transform your problem from a system that deadlocks to a system that livelocks. However, in large systems, because there are more moving parts, there is a higher probability that your system will experience a different timing profile than when you deadlocked last. Therefore, it is preferable to chance a livelock and fix that as time permits, than for a deadlock to occur and have a system recoverable only by restart.

Note that this isn't a recommendation for how to build a system correctly; rather a suggestion for building a system that is tolerant to timing errors you may not have exercised during development and testing. I do recommend you keep the timeouts in place, but the goal should be to converge on a system without deadlocks where the timeouts are never triggered.

Now that we have a grasp on when to utilize timeouts, let's turn our attention to the causes of cancellation, and how to build a concurrent process to handle cancellation gracefully. There are a number of reasons why a concurrent process might be canceled:

Timeouts
A timeout is an implicit cancellation.

User intervention
For a good user experience, it's usually advisable to start long-running processes concurrently and then report status back to the user at a polling interval, or allow the users to query for status as they see fit. When there are user-facing concurrent operations, it is therefore also sometimes necessary to allow the users to cancel the operation they've started.

Parent cancellation
For that matter, if any kind of parent of a concurrent operation—human or otherwise—stops, as a child of that parent, we will be canceled.

Replicated requests
We may wish to send data to multiple concurrent processes in an attempt to get a faster response from one of them. When the first one comes back, we would want to cancel the rest of the processes. We'll discuss this in detail in the section "Replicated Requests" on page 172.

There are likely other possible reasons, too. However, the question "why" is not nearly as difficult or interesting as the question of "how." In Chapter 4 we explored two ways to cancel concurrent processes: a done channel, and the context.Context type. But that's the easy part; here we want to explore more complex questions: when a concurrent process is canceled, what does that mean for the algorithm that was executing, and its downstream consumers? When writing concurrent code that can be terminated at any time, what things do you need to take into account?

In order to answer those questions, the first thing we need to explore is the preemptability of a concurrent process. Take the following code, and assume it's running in its own goroutine:

```
var value interface{}
select {
case <-done:
    return
case value = <-valueStream:
}

result := reallyLongCalculation(value)

select {
case <-done:
    return
case resultStream<-result:
}
```

We've dutifully coupled the read from `valueStream` and the write to `resultStream`
with a check against the done channel to see if the goroutine has been canceled, but
we still have a problem. `reallyLongCalculation` doesn't look to be preemptable, and,
according to the name, it looks like it might take a really long time! This means that if
something attempts to cancel this goroutine while `reallyLongCalculation` is executing, it could be a very long time before we acknowledge the cancellation and halt.
Let's try and make `reallyLongCaluclation` preemptable and see what happens:

```
reallyLongCalculation := func(
    done <-chan interface{},
    value interface{},
) interface{} {
    intermediateResult := longCalculation(value)
    select {
    case <-done:
        return nil
    default:
    }

    return longCaluclation(intermediateResult)
}
```

We've made some progress: `reallyLongCaluclation` is now preemptable, but we can
see that we've only halved the problem: we can only preempt `reallyLongCalcula`
`tion` in between calls to other, seemingly long-running, function calls. To solve this,
we need to make `longCalculation` preemptable as well:

```
reallyLongCalculation := func(
    done <-chan interface{},
    value interface{},
) interface{} {
    intermediateResult := longCalculation(done, value)
    return longCaluclation(done, intermediateResult)
}
```

If you take this line of reasoning to its logical conclusion, we see that we must do two things: define the period within which our concurrent process is preemptable, and ensure that any functionality that takes more time than this period is itself preemptable. An easy way to do this is to break up the pieces of your goroutine into smaller pieces. You should aim for all *nonpreemptable* atomic operations to complete in less time than the period you've deemed acceptable.

there's another problem lurking here as well: if our goroutine happens to modify shared state—e.g., a database, a file, an in-memory data structure—what happens when the goroutine is canceled? Does your goroutine try and roll back the intermediary work it's done? How long does it have to do this work? Something has told the goroutine that it should halt, so the goroutine shouldn't take too long to roll back its work, right?

It's difficult to give general advice on how to handle this problem because the nature of your algorithm will dictate so much of how you handle this situation; however, if you keep your modifications to any shared state within a tight scope, and/or ensure those modifications are easily rolled back, you can usually handle cancellations pretty well. If possible, build up intermediate results in-memory and then modify state as quickly as possible. As an example, here is the *wrong* way to do it:

```
result := add(1, 2, 3)
writeTallyToState(result)
result = add(result, 4, 5, 6)
writeTallyToState(result)
result = add(result, 7, 8, 9)
writeTallyToState(result)
```

Here we write to state three times. If a goroutine running this code were canceled before the final write, we'd need to somehow roll back the previous two calls to `write TallyToState`. Contrast that approach with this:

```
result := add(1, 2, 3, 4, 5, 6, 7, 8, 9)
writeTallyToState(result)
```

Here the surface area we have to worry about rolling back is much smaller. If the cancellation comes in after our call to `writeToState`, we still need a way to back out our changes, but the probability that this will happen is much smaller since we only modify state once.

Another issue you need to be concerned with is duplicated messages. Let's say you have a pipeline with three stages: a generator stage, stage A, and stage B. The generator stage monitors stage A by keeping track of how long it's been since it last read from its channel, and brings up a new instance, A2, if the current instance becomes nonperformant. If that were to happen, it is possible for stage B to receive duplicate messages (Figure 5-1).

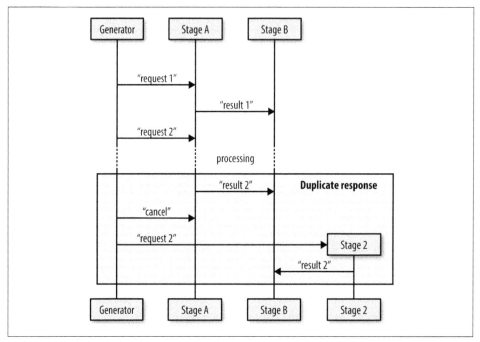

Figure 5-1. Example of how a duplicate message could occur

You can see here that it's possible for stage B to receive duplicate messages if the cancellation message comes in after stage A has already sent its result to stage B.

There are a few ways to avoid sending duplicate messages. The easiest (and the method I recommend) is to make it vanishingly unlikely that a parent goroutine will send a cancellation signal after a child goroutine has already reported a result. This requires bidirectional communication between the stages, and we'll cover this in detail in the section "Heartbeats" on page 161. Other approaches are:

Accept either the first or last result reported
    If your algorithm allows it, or your concurrent process is idempotent, you can simply allow for the possibility of duplicate messages in your downstream processes and choose whether to accept the first or last message you receive.

Poll the parent goroutine for permission
    You can use bidirectional communication with your parent to explicitly request permission to send your message. As we'll see, this approach is similar to heartbeats. It would look something like Figure 5-2.

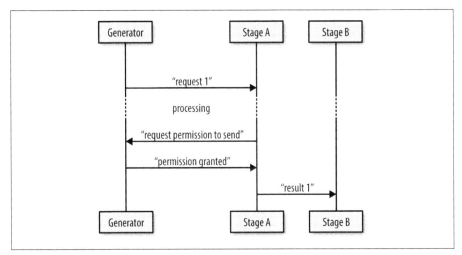

Figure 5-2. An example of polling the parent goroutine

Because we explicitly request permission to perform the write to B's channel, this is an even safer route than heartbeats; however, in practice, this is rarely necessary, and since it is more complicated than heartbeats, and heartbeats are more generally useful, I suggest you just use heartbeats.

When designing your concurrent processes, be sure to take into account timeouts and cancellation. Like many other topics in software engineering, neglecting timeouts and cancellation from the beginning and then attempting to put them in later is a bit like trying to add eggs to a cake after it has been baked.

Heartbeats

Heartbeats are a way for concurrent processes to signal life to outside parties. They get their name from human anatomy wherein a heartbeat signifies life to an observer. Heartbeats have been around since before Go, and remain useful within it.

There are a few different reasons heartbeats are interesting for concurrent code. They allow us insights into our system, and they can make testing the system deterministic when it might otherwise not be.

There are two different types of heartbeats we'll discuss in this section:

- Heartbeats that occur on a time interval.
- Heartbeats that occur at the beginning of a unit of work.

Heartbeats that occur on a time interval are useful for concurrent code that might be waiting for something else to happen for it to process a unit of work. Because you don't know when that work might come in, your goroutine might be sitting around for a while waiting for something to happen. A heartbeat is a way to signal to its listeners that everything is well, and that the silence is expected.

The following code demonstrates a goroutine that exposes a heartbeat:

```
doWork := func(
    done <-chan interface{},
    pulseInterval time.Duration,
) (<-chan interface{}, <-chan time.Time) {
    heartbeat := make(chan interface{}) ❶
    results := make(chan time.Time)
    go func() {
        defer close(heartbeat)
        defer close(results)

        pulse := time.Tick(pulseInterval) ❷
        workGen := time.Tick(2*pulseInterval) ❸

        sendPulse := func() {
            select {
            case heartbeat <-struct{}{}:
            default: ❹
            }
        }
        sendResult := func(r time.Time) {
            for {
                select {
                case <-done:
                    return
                case <-pulse: ❺
                    sendPulse()
                case results <- r:
                    return
                }
            }
        }

        for {
            select {
            case <-done:
                return
            case <-pulse: ❺
                sendPulse()
            case r := <-workGen:
                sendResult(r)
            }
        }
    }()
    return heartbeat, results
}
```

❶ Here we set up a channel to send heartbeats on. We return this out of doWork.

❷ Here we set the heartbeat to pulse at the pulseInterval we were given. Every pulseInterval there will be something to read on this channel.

❸ This is just another ticker used to simulate work coming in. We choose a duration greater than the pulseInterval so that we can see some heartbeats coming out of the goroutine.

❹ Note that we include a default clause. We must always guard against the fact that no one may be listening to our heartbeat. The results emitted from the goroutine are critical, but the pulses are not.

❺ Just like with done channels, anytime you perform a send or receive, you also need to include a case for the heartbeat's pulse.

Notice that because we might be sending out multiple pulses while we wait for input, or multiple pulses while waiting to send results, all the select statements need to be within for loops. Looking good so far; how do we utilize this function and consume the events it emits? Let's take a look:

```go
done := make(chan interface{})
time.AfterFunc(10*time.Second, func() { close(done) }) ❶

const timeout = 2*time.Second ❷
heartbeat, results := doWork(done, timeout/2) ❸
for {
    select {
    case _, ok := <-heartbeat: ❹
        if ok == false {
            return
        }
        fmt.Println("pulse")
    case r, ok := <-results: ❺
        if ok == false {
            return
        }
        fmt.Printf("results %v\n", r.Second())
    case <-time.After(timeout): ❻
        return
    }
}
```

❶ We set up the standard done channel and close it after 10 seconds. This gives our goroutine time to do some work.

❷ Here we set our timeout period. We'll use this to couple our heartbeat interval to our timeout.

❸ We pass in `timeout/2` here. This gives our heartbeat an extra tick to respond so that our timeout isn't too sensitive.

❹ Here we select on the heartbeat. When there are no results, we are at least guaranteed a message from the `heartbeat` channel every `timeout/2`. If we don't receive it, we know there's something wrong with the goroutine itself.

❺ Here we select from the results channel; nothing fancy going on here.

❻ Here we time out if we haven't received either a heartbeat or a new result.

Running this code produces:

```
pulse
pulse
results 52
pulse
pulse
results 54
pulse
pulse
results 56
pulse
pulse
results 58
pulse
```

You can see that we receive about two pulses per result as we intended.

Now in a properly functioning system, heartbeats aren't that interesting. We might use them to gather statistics regarding idle time, but the utility for interval-based heartbeats really shines when your goroutine isn't behaving as expected.

Consider the next example. We'll simulate an incorrectly written goroutine with a panic by stopping the goroutine after only two iterations, and then not closing either of our channels. Let's have a look:

```go
doWork := func(
    done <-chan interface{},
    pulseInterval time.Duration,
) (<-chan interface{}, <-chan time.Time) {
    heartbeat := make(chan interface{})
    results := make(chan time.Time)
    go func() {
        pulse := time.Tick(pulseInterval)
        workGen := time.Tick(2*pulseInterval)
```

```
        sendPulse := func() {
            select {
            case heartbeat <-struct{}{}:
            default:
            }
        }
        sendResult := func(r time.Time) {
            for {
                select {
                case <-pulse:
                    sendPulse()
                case results <- r:
                    return
                }
            }
        }

        for i := 0; i < 2; i++ { ❶
            select {
            case <-done:
                return
            case <-pulse:
                sendPulse()
            case r := <-workGen:
                sendResult(r)
            }
        }
    }()
    return heartbeat, results
}

done := make(chan interface{})
time.AfterFunc(10*time.Second, func() { close(done) })

const timeout = 2 * time.Second
heartbeat, results := doWork(done, timeout/2)
for {
    select {
    case _, ok := <-heartbeat:
        if ok == false {
            return
        }
        fmt.Println("pulse")
    case r, ok := <-results:
        if ok == false {
            return
        }
        fmt.Printf("results %v\n", r)
    case <-time.After(timeout):
        fmt.Println("worker goroutine is not healthy!")
        return
```

```
        }
    }
```

❶ Here is our simulated panic. Instead of infinitely looping until we're asked to stop, as in the previous example, we'll only loop twice.

Running this code produces:

```
pulse
pulse
worker goroutine is not healthy!
```

Beautiful! Within two seconds our system realizes something is amiss with our goroutine and breaks the for-select loop. By using a heartbeat, we have successfully avoided a deadlock, and we remain deterministic by not having to rely on a longer timeout. We'll discuss how we can take this concept even further in "Healing Unhealthy Goroutines" on page 188.

Also note that heartbeats help with the opposite case: they let us know that long-running goroutines remain up, but are just taking a while to produce a value to send on the values channel.

Now let's shift over to looking at heartbeats that occur at the beginning of a unit of work. These are extremely useful for tests. Here's an example that sends a pulse before every unit of work:

```
doWork := func(done <-chan interface{}) (<-chan interface{}, <-chan int) {
    heartbeatStream := make(chan interface{}, 1) ❶
    workStream := make(chan int)
    go func () {
        defer close(heartbeatStream)
        defer close(workStream)

        for i := 0; i < 10; i++ {
            select { ❷
            case heartbeatStream <- struct{}{}:
            default: ❸
            }

            select {
            case <-done:
                return
            case workStream <- rand.Intn(10):
            }
        }
    }()

    return heartbeatStream, workStream
}

done := make(chan interface{})
```

```
    defer close(done)

    heartbeat, results := doWork(done)
    for {
        select {
        case _, ok := <-heartbeat:
            if ok {
                fmt.Println("pulse")
            } else {
                return
            }
        case r, ok := <-results:
            if ok {
                fmt.Printf("results %v\n", r)
            } else {
                return
            }
        }
    }
}
```

❶ Here we create the heartbeat channel with a buffer of one. This ensures that there's always at least one pulse sent out even if no one is listening in time for the send to occur.

❷ Here we set up a separate select block for the heartbeat. We don't want to include this in the same select block as the send on results because if the receiver isn't ready for the result, they'll receive a pulse instead, and the current value of the result will be lost. We also don't include a case statement for the done channel since we have a default case that will just fall through.

❸ Once again we guard against the fact that no one may be listening to our heartbeats. Because our heartbeat channel was created with a buffer of one, if someone *is* listening, but not in time for the first pulse, they'll still be notified of a pulse.

Running this code produces:

```
pulse
results 1
pulse
results 7
pulse
results 7
pulse
results 9
pulse
results 1
pulse
results 8
```

```
pulse
results 5
pulse
results 0
pulse
results 6
pulse
results 0
```

You can see in this example that we receive one pulse for every result, as intended.

Where this technique really shines is in writing tests. Interval-based heartbeats can be used in the same fashion, but if you only care that the goroutine has started doing its work, this style of heartbeat is simple. Consider the following snippet of code:

```
func DoWork(
    done <-chan interface{},
    nums ...int,
) (<-chan interface{}, <-chan int) {
    heartbeat := make(chan interface{}, 1)
    intStream := make(chan int)
    go func() {
        defer close(heartbeat)
        defer close(intStream)

        time.Sleep(2*time.Second) ❶

        for _, n := range nums {
            select {
            case heartbeat <- struct{}{}:
            default:
            }

            select {
            case <-done:
                return
            case intStream <- n:
            }
        }
    }()

    return heartbeat, intStream
}
```

❶ Here we simulate some kind of delay before the goroutine can begin working. In practice this can be all kinds of things and is nondeterministic. I've seen delays caused by CPU load, disk contention, network latency, and goblins.

The DoWork function is a pretty simple generator that converts the numbers we pass in to a stream on the channel it returns. Let's try testing this function. Here's an example of a *bad* test:

```
func TestDoWork_GeneratesAllNumbers(t *testing.T) {
    done := make(chan interface{})
    defer close(done)

    intSlice := []int{0, 1, 2, 3, 5}
    _, results := DoWork(done, intSlice...)

    for i, expected := range intSlice {
        select {
        case r := <-results:
            if r != expected {
                t.Errorf(
                    "index %v: expected %v, but received %v,",
                    i,
                    expected,
                    r,
                )
            }
        case <-time.After(1 * time.Second): ❶
            t.Fatal("test timed out")
        }
    }
}
```

❶ Here we time out after what we think is a reasonable duration to prevent a broken goroutine from deadlocking our test.

Running this test produces:

```
go test ./bad_concurrent_test.go
--- FAIL: TestDoWork_GeneratesAllNumbers (1.00s)
    bad_concurrent_test.go:46: test timed out
FAIL
FAIL    command-line-arguments  1.002s
```

This test is bad because it's nondeterministic. In our example function, I've ensured this test will always fail, but if I were to remove the time.Sleep, the situation actually gets worse: this test will pass at times, and fail at others.

We mentioned earlier how factors external to the process can cause the goroutine to take longer to get to its first iteration. Even whether or not the goroutine is scheduled in the first place is a concern. The point is that we can't be guaranteed that the first iteration of the goroutine will occur before our timeout is reached, and so we begin thinking in terms of probabilities: how likely is it that this timeout will be significant? We could increase the timeout, but that means failures will take a long time, thereby slowing down our test suite.

This is an awful, awful position to be in. The team no longer knows whether it can trust a test failure and begin ignoring failures—the whole endeavor begins to unravel.

Fortunately with a heartbeat this is easily solved. Here is a test that is deterministic:

```go
func TestDoWork_GeneratesAllNumbers(t *testing.T) {
    done := make(chan interface{})
    defer close(done)

    intSlice := []int{0, 1, 2, 3, 5}
    heartbeat, results := DoWork(done, intSlice...)

    <-heartbeat ❶

    i := 0
    for r := range results {
        if expected := intSlice[i]; r != expected {
            t.Errorf("index %v: expected %v, but received %v,", i, expected, r)
        }
        i++
    }
}
```

❶ Here we wait for the goroutine to signal that it's beginning to process an iteration.

Running this test produces the following output:

```
ok      command-line-arguments                          2.002s
```

Because of the heartbeat, we can safely write our test without timeouts. The only risk we run is of one of our iterations taking an inordinate amount of time. If that's important to us, we can utilize the safer interval-based heartbeats and achieve perfect safety.

Here is an example of a test utilizing interval-based heartbeats:

```go
func DoWork(
    done <-chan interface{},
    pulseInterval time.Duration,
    nums ...int,
) (<-chan interface{}, <-chan int) {
    heartbeat := make(chan interface{}, 1)
    intStream := make(chan int)
    go func() {
        defer close(heartbeat)
        defer close(intStream)

        time.Sleep(2*time.Second)

        pulse := time.Tick(pulseInterval)
    numLoop: ❷
        for _, n := range nums {
            for { ❶
                select {
                case <-done:
                    return
```

```
                    case <-pulse:
                        select {
                        case heartbeat <- struct{}{}:
                        default:
                        }
                    case intStream <- n:
                        continue numLoop ❸
                    }
                }
            }
        }()

        return heartbeat, intStream
    }

    func TestDoWork_GeneratesAllNumbers(t *testing.T) {
        done := make(chan interface{})
        defer close(done)

        intSlice := []int{0, 1, 2, 3, 5}
        const timeout = 2*time.Second
        heartbeat, results := DoWork(done, timeout/2, intSlice...)

        <-heartbeat ❹

        i := 0
        for {
            select {
            case r, ok := <-results:
                if ok == false {
                    return
                } else if expected := intSlice[i]; r != expected {
                    t.Errorf(
                        "index %v: expected %v, but received %v,",
                        i,
                        expected,
                        r,
                    )
                }
                i++
            case <-heartbeat: ❺
            case <-time.After(timeout):
                t.Fatal("test timed out")
            }
        }
    }
```

❶ We require two loops: one to range over our list of numbers, and this inner loop to run until the number is successfully sent on the intStream.

❷ We're using a label here to make continuing from the inner loop a little simpler.

❸ Here we continue executing the outer loop.

❹ We still wait for the first heartbeat to occur to indicate we've entered the goroutine's loop.

❺ We also select on the heartbeat here to keep the timeout from occuring.

Running this test produces:

```
ok      command-line-arguments                                          3.002s
```

You've probably noticed that this version of the test is much less clear. The logic of what we're testing is a bit muddled. For this reason—if you're reasonably sure the goroutine's loop won't stop executing once it's started—I recommend only blocking on the first heartbeat and then falling into a simple range statement. You can write separate tests that specifically test for failing to close channels, loop iterations taking too long, and any other timing-related issues.

Heartbeats aren't strictly necessary when writing concurrent code, but this section demonstrates their utility. For any long-running goroutines, or goroutines that need to be tested, I highly recommend this pattern.

Replicated Requests

For some applications, receiving a response as quickly as possible is the top priority. For example, maybe the application is servicing a user's HTTP request, or retrieving a replicated blob of data. In these instances you can make a trade-off: you can replicate the request to multiple handlers (whether those be goroutines, processes, or servers), and one of them will return faster than the other ones; you can then immediately return the result. The downside is that you'll have to utilize resources to keep multiple copies of the handlers running.

If this replication is done in-memory, it might not be that costly, but if replicating the handlers requires replicating processes, servers, or even data centers, this can become quite costly. The decision you'll have to make is whether or not the cost is worth the benefit.

Let's look at how you can replicate requests within a single process. We'll use multiple goroutines to serve as request handlers, and the goroutines will sleep for a random amount of time between one and six nanoseconds to simulate load. This will give us handlers that return a result at various times and will allow us to see how this can lead to faster results.

Here's an example that replicates a simulated request over 10 handlers:

```
doWork := func(
    done <-chan interface{},
    id int,
    wg *sync.WaitGroup,
    result chan<- int,
) {
    started := time.Now()
    defer wg.Done()

    // Simulate random load
    simulatedLoadTime := time.Duration(1+rand.Intn(5))*time.Second
    select {
    case <-done:
    case <-time.After(simulatedLoadTime):
    }

    select {
    case <-done:
    case result <- id:
    }

    took := time.Since(started)
    // Display how long handlers would have taken
    if took < simulatedLoadTime {
        took = simulatedLoadTime
    }
    fmt.Printf("%v took %v\n", id, took)
}

done := make(chan interface{})
result := make(chan int)

var wg sync.WaitGroup
wg.Add(10)

for i:=0; i < 10; i++ { ❶
    go doWork(done, i, &wg, result)
}

firstReturned := <-result ❷
close(done) ❸
wg.Wait()

fmt.Printf("Received an answer from #%v\n", firstReturned)
```

❶ Here we start 10 handlers to handle our requests.

❷ This line grabs the first returned value from the group of handlers.

❸ Here we cancel all the remaining handlers. This ensures they don't continue to do
    unnecessary work.

Running this code produces:

```
8 took 1.000211046s
4 took 3s
9 took 2s
1 took 1.000568933s
7 took 2s
3 took 1.000590992s
5 took 5s
0 took 3s
6 took 4s
2 took 2s
Received an answer from #8
```

In this run, it looks like handler #8 returned fastest. Note that in the output we're displaying how long each handler *would* have taken so that you can get a sense of how much time this technique can save. Imagine if you only spun up one handler and it happened to be handler #5. Instead of waiting just over a second for the request to be handled, you would have had to wait for five seconds.

The only caveat to this approach is that all of your handlers need to have equal opportunity to service the request. In other words, you're not going to have a chance at receiving the fastest time from a handler that *can't* service the request. As I mentioned, whatever resources the handlers are using to do their job need to be replicated as well.

A different symptom of the same problem is uniformity. If your handlers are too much alike, the chances that any one will be an outlier is smaller. You should only replicate out requests like this to handlers that have different runtime conditions: different processes, machines, paths to a data store, or access to different data stores altogether.

Although this is can be expensive to set up and maintain, if speed is your goal, this is a valuable technique. In addition, this naturally provides fault tolerance and scalability.

Rate Limiting

If you've ever worked with an API for a service, you've likely had to contend with rate limiting, which constrains the number of times some kind of resource is accessed to some finite number per unit of time. The resource can be anything: API connections, disk reads/writes, network packets, errors.

Have you ever wondered why services put rate limits in place? Why not allow unfettered access to a system? The most obvious answer is that by rate limiting a system, you prevent entire classes of attack vectors against your system. If malicious users can access your system as quickly as their resources allow it, they can do all kinds of things.

For example, they could fill up your service's disk either with log messages or valid requests. If you've misconfigured your log rotation, they could even perform something malicious and then make enough requests that any record of the activity would be rotated out of the log and into `/dev/null`. They could attempt to brute-force access to a resource, or maybe they would just perform a distributed denial of service attack. The point is: if you don't rate limit requests to your system, you cannot easily secure it.

Malicious use isn't the only reason. In distributed systems, a legitimate user could degrade the performance of the system for other users if they're performing operations at a high enough volume, or if the code they're exercising is buggy. This can even cause the death-spirals we discussed earlier. From a product standpoint, this is awful! Usually you want to make some kind of guarantees to your users about what kind of performance they can expect on a consistent basis. If one user can affect that agreement, you're in for a bad time. A user's mental model is usually that their access to the system is sandboxed and can neither affect nor be affected by other users' activities. If you break that mental model, your system can feel like it's not well engineered, and even cause users to become angry or leave.

Even with only *one* user, rate limits can be advantageous. A lot of the time, systems have been developed to work well under the common use case, but may begin behaving differently under different circumstances. In complicated systems such as distributed systems, this effect can cascade through the system and have drastic, unintended consequences. Maybe under load you begin dropping packets, which causes your distributed database to lose its quorum and stop accepting writes, which causes your existing requests to fail, which causes... You can see how this can be a bad thing. It isn't unheard of for systems to perform a kind of DDoS attack on themselves in these instances!

A Story from the Field

I once worked on a distributed system that scaled work in parallel by starting new processes (this allowed it to scale horizontally to multiple machines). Each process would open a database connection, read some data, and do some calculations. For a time, we had great success in scaling the system in this manner to meet the needs of clients. However, after a while the system utilization grew to a point where reads from the database were timing out.

Our database administrators pored over logs to try and figure out what was going wrong. In the end, they discovered that because there were no rate limits set for anything on the system, processes were stomping all over each other. Disk contention would spike to 100% and remain there as different processes attempted to read data from different parts of the disk. This in turn led to a kind of sadistic round-robin timeout-retry loop. Jobs would never complete.

> A system was devised to place limits on the number of connections possible on the database, and rate limits were placed on bits per second a connection could read, and the problems went away. Clients had to wait longer for their jobs to complete, but they completed, and we were able to perform proper capacity planning to expand the capacity of the system in a structured way.

Rate limits allow you to reason about the performance and stability of your system by preventing it from falling outside the boundaries you've already investigated. If you need to expand those boundaries, you can do so in a controlled manner after lots of testing and coffee.

In scenarios where you're charging for access to your system, rate limits can maintain a healthy relationship with your clients. You can allow them to try the system out under heavily constrained rate limits. Google does this with its cloud offerings to great success.

After they've become paying customers, rate limits can even *protect* your users. Because most of the time access to the system is programmatic, it's very easy to introduce a bug that accesses your paid system in a runaway manner. This can be a *very* costly mistake and leaves both parties in the awkward situation of deciding what to do: does the service owner eat the cost and forgive the unintended access, or is the user forced to pay the bill, which might sour the relationship permanently?

Rate limits are often thought of from the perspective of people who *build* the resources being limited, but rate limiting can also be utilized by users. If I'm only just understanding how to utilize a service's API, it would be very comforting to be able to scale the rate limits way down so I know I won't shoot myself in the foot.

Hopefully I've given enough justification to convince you that rate limits are good even if you set limits that you think will never be reached. They're pretty simple to create, and they solve so many problems that it's hard to rationalize *not* using them.

So how do we go about implementing rate limits in Go?

Most rate limiting is done by utilizing an algorithm called the *token bucket*. It's very easy to understand, and relatively easy to implement as well. Let's take a look at the theory behind it.

Let's assume that to utilize a resource, you have to have an *access token* for the resource. Without the token, your request is denied. Now imagine these tokens are stored in a bucket waiting to be retrieved for usage. The bucket has a depth of d, which indicates it can hold d access tokens at a time. For example, if the bucket has a depth of five, it can hold five tokens.

Now, every time you need to access a resource, you reach into the bucket and remove a token. If your bucket contains five tokens, and you access the resource five times, you'd be able to do so; but on the sixth try, no access token would be available. You either have to queue your request until a token becomes available, or deny the request.

Here's a time table to help visualize the concept. `time` represents the time-delta in seconds, `bucket` represents the number of request tokens in the bucket, and a `tok` in the `request` column denotes a successful request. (In this and future time tables, we'll assume the requests are instantaneous to simplify the visualization.)

time	bucket	request
0	5	tok
0	4	tok
0	3	tok
0	2	tok
0	1	tok
0	0	
1	0	
	0	

You can see that we're able to make all five requests before the first second, and then we are blocked as no more tokens are available for use.

So far, this is pretty straightforward. What about replenishing the tokens; do we ever get new ones? In the token bucket algorithm, we define r to be the rate at which tokens are added *back* to the bucket. It can be one a nanosecond, or one a minute. This becomes what we commonly think of as the rate limit: because we have to wait until new tokens become available, we limit our operations to that refresh rate.

Here's an example of a token bucket with a depth of one, and a rate of 1 tokens/ second:

time	bucket	request
0	1	
0	0	tok
1	0	
2	1	
2	0	tok
3	0	
4	1	
4	0	tok

You can see that we're immediately able to make a request, but we are then limited to one request every other second. Our rate limitation is working beautifully!

So we now have two settings we can fiddle with: how many tokens are available for immediate use—d, the depth of the bucket—and the rate at which they are replenished—r. Between these two we can control both the *burstiness* and overall rate limit. Burstiness simply means how many requests can be made when the bucket is full.

Here's an example of a token bucket with a depth of five, and a rate of `0.5` tokens/ second:

time	bucket	request
0	5	
0	4	tok
0	3	tok
0	2	tok
0	1	tok
0	0	tok
1	0 (0.5)	
2	1	
2	0	tok
3	0 (0.5)	
4	1	
4	0	tok

Here, we were able to immediately make five requests, after which point we were limited to a request every two seconds. Our *burst* was at the beginning.

Be aware that users may not consume the entire bucket of tokens in one long stream. The depth of the bucket only controls the bucket's capacity. Here's an example of a user who had a burst of two, and then four seconds later, had a burst of five:

time	bucket	request
0	5	
0	4	tok
0	3	tok
1	3	
2	4	
3	5	
4	5	
5	4	tok

time	bucket	request
5	3	tok
5	2	tok
5	1	tok
5	0	tok

While a user has tokens available, burstiness allows access to the system constrained only by the capabilities of the caller. For users who only access the system intermittently, but want to round-trip as quickly as possible when they do, bursts are nice to have. You just need to either ensure your system can handle all users bursting at once, or that it is statistically improbable that enough users will burst at the same time to affect your system. Either way, a rate limit allows you to take a calculated risk.

Let's put this algorithm to use and see how a Go program might behave when written against an implementation of the token bucket algorithm.

Let's pretend we have access to an API, and a Go client has been provided to utilize it. This API has two endpoints: one for reading a file, and one for resolving a domain name to an IP address. For simplicity's sake, I'm going to leave off any arguments and return values that would be needed to actually access a service. So here's our client:

```go
func Open() *APIConnection {
    return &APIConnection{}
}

type APIConnection struct {}

func (a *APIConnection) ReadFile(ctx context.Context) error {
    // Pretend we do work here
    return nil
}

func (a *APIConnection) ResolveAddress(ctx context.Context) error {
    // Pretend we do work here
    return nil
}
```

Since in theory this request is going over the wire, we take a context.Context in as the first argument in case we need to cancel the request or pass values over to the server. Pretty standard stuff.

We'll now create a simple driver to access this API. The driver needs to read 10 files and resolve 10 addresses, but the files and addresses have no relation to each other and so the driver can make these API calls concurrent to one another. Later this will help stress our APIClient and exercise our rate limiter.

```go
func main() {
    defer log.Printf("Done.")
```

```
        log.SetOutput(os.Stdout)
        log.SetFlags(log.Ltime | log.LUTC)

        apiConnection := Open()
        var wg sync.WaitGroup
        wg.Add(20)

        for i := 0; i < 10; i++ {
            go func() {
                defer wg.Done()
                err := apiConnection.ReadFile(context.Background())
                if err != nil {
                    log.Printf("cannot ReadFile: %v", err)
                }
                log.Printf("ReadFile")
            }()
        }

        for i := 0; i < 10; i++ {
            go func() {
                defer wg.Done()
                err := apiConnection.ResolveAddress(context.Background())
                if err != nil {
                    log.Printf("cannot ResolveAddress: %v", err)
                }
                log.Printf("ResolveAddress")
            }()
        }

        wg.Wait()
    }
```

Running this code produces:

```
20:13:13 ResolveAddress
20:13:13 ReadFile
20:13:13 ResolveAddress
20:13:13 ReadFile
20:13:13 ReadFile
20:13:13 ReadFile
20:13:13 ReadFile
20:13:13 ResolveAddress
20:13:13 ResolveAddress
20:13:13 ReadFile
20:13:13 ResolveAddress
20:13:13 ResolveAddress
20:13:13 ResolveAddress
20:13:13 ResolveAddress
20:13:13 ResolveAddress
20:13:13 ResolveAddress
20:13:13 ReadFile
20:13:13 ReadFile
20:13:13 ReadFile
```

```
20:13:13 ReadFile
20:13:13 Done.
```

We can see that all API requests are fielded almost simultaneously. We have no rate limiting set up and so our clients are free to access the system as frequently as they like. Now is a good time to remind you that a bug could exist in our driver that could result in an infinite loop. Without rate limiting, I could be staring down a nasty bill.

OK, so let's introduce a rate limiter! I'm going to do so within the APIConnection, but normally a rate limiter would be running on a server so the users couldn't trivially bypass it. Production systems might *also* include a client-side rate limiter to help prevent the client from making unnecessary calls only to be denied, but that is an optimization. For our purposes, a client-side rate limiter keeps things simple.

We're going to be looking at examples that use an implementation of a token bucket rate limiter from the golang.org/x/time/rate package. I chose this package because this is as close to the standard library as I could get. There are certainly other packages out there that do the same thing with more bells and whistles, and those may serve you better for use in production systems. The golang.org/x/time/rate package is pretty simple, so it should work well for our purposes.

The first two ways we'll interact with this package are the Limit type and the NewLimiter function, defined here:

```
// Limit defines the maximum frequency of some events.  Limit is
// represented as number of events per second.  A zero Limit allows no
// events.
type Limit float64

// NewLimiter returns a new Limiter that allows events up to rate r
// and permits bursts of at most b tokens.
func NewLimiter(r Limit, b int) *Limiter
```

In NewLimiter, we see two familiar parameters: r and b. r is the rate we discussed previously, and b is the bucket depth we discussed.

The rates package also defines a helper method, Every, to assist in converting a time.Duration into a Limit:

```
// Every converts a minimum time interval between events to a Limit.
func Every(interval time.Duration) Limit
```

The Every function makes sense, but I want to discuss rate limits in terms of the number of operations per time measurement, not the interval between requests. We can express this as the following:

```
rate.Limit(events/timePeriod.Seconds())
```

But I don't want to type that every time, and the Every function has some special logic that will return rate.Inf—an indication that there is no limit—if the interval provided is zero. Because of this, we'll express our helper function in terms of the Every function:

```
func Per(eventCount int, duration time.Duration) rate.Limit {
    return rate.Every(duration/time.Duration(eventCount))
}
```

After we create a `rate.Limiter`, we'll want to use it to block our requests until we're given an access token. We can do that with the `Wait` method, which simply calls `WaitN` with an argument of 1:

```
// Wait is shorthand for WaitN(ctx, 1).
func (lim *Limiter) Wait(ctx context.Context)

// WaitN blocks until lim permits n events to happen.
// It returns an error if n exceeds the Limiter's burst size, the Context is
// canceled, or the expected wait time exceeds the Context's Deadline.
func (lim *Limiter) WaitN(ctx context.Context, n int) (err error)
```

We should now have all the ingredients we'll need to begin rate limiting our API requests. Let's modify our `APIConnection` type and give it a try!

```
func Open() *APIConnection {
    return &APIConnection{
        rateLimiter: rate.NewLimiter(rate.Limit(1), 1), ❶
    }
}

type APIConnection struct {
    rateLimiter *rate.Limiter
}

func (a *APIConnection) ReadFile(ctx context.Context) error {
    if err := a.rateLimiter.Wait(ctx); err != nil { ❷
        return err
    }
    // Pretend we do work here
    return nil
}

func (a *APIConnection) ResolveAddress(ctx context.Context) error {
    if err := a.rateLimiter.Wait(ctx); err != nil { ❷
        return err
    }
    // Pretend we do work here
    return nil
}
```

❶ Here we set the rate limit for all API connections to one event per second.

❷ Here we wait on the rate limiter to have enough access tokens for us to complete our request.

Running this code produces:

```
22:08:30 ResolveAddress
22:08:31 ReadFile
22:08:32 ReadFile
22:08:33 ReadFile
22:08:34 ResolveAddress
22:08:35 ResolveAddress
22:08:36 ResolveAddress
22:08:37 ResolveAddress
22:08:38 ResolveAddress
22:08:39 ReadFile
22:08:40 ResolveAddress
22:08:41 ResolveAddress
22:08:42 ResolveAddress
22:08:43 ResolveAddress
22:08:44 ReadFile
22:08:45 ReadFile
22:08:46 ReadFile
22:08:47 ReadFile
22:08:48 ReadFile
22:08:49 ReadFile
22:08:49 Done.
```

You can see that whereas before we were fielding all of our API requests simultaneously, we're now completing a request once a second. It looks like our rate limiter is working!

This gets us very basic rate limiting, but in production we're likely going to want something a little more complex. We will probably want to establish multiple tiers of limits: fine-grained controls to limit requests per second, and coarse-grained controls to limit requests per minute, hour, or day.

In certain instances, it's possible to do this with a single rate limiter; however, it's not possible in all cases, and by attempting to roll the semantics of limits per unit of time into a single layer, you lose a lot of information around the intent of the rate limiter. For these reasons, I find it easier to keep the limiters separate and then combine them into one rate limiter that manages the interaction for you. To this end I've created a simple aggregate rate limiter called multiLimiter. Here is the definition:

```
type RateLimiter interface { ❶
    Wait(context.Context) error
    Limit() rate.Limit
}

func MultiLimiter(limiters ...RateLimiter) *multiLimiter {
    byLimit := func(i, j int) bool {
        return limiters[i].Limit() < limiters[j].Limit()
    }
    sort.Slice(limiters, byLimit) ❷
    return &multiLimiter{limiters: limiters}
```

```
    }

    type multiLimiter struct {
        limiters []RateLimiter
    }

    func (l *multiLimiter) Wait(ctx context.Context) error {
        for _, l := range l.limiters {
            if err := l.Wait(ctx); err != nil {
                return err
            }
        }
        return nil
    }

    func (l *multiLimiter) Limit() rate.Limit {
        return l.limiters[0].Limit()  ❸
    }
```

❶ Here we define a `RateLimiter` interface so that a `MultiLimiter` can recursively define other `MultiLimiter` instances.

❷ Here we implement an optimization and sort by the `Limit()` of each `RateLimiter`.

❸ Because we sort the child `RateLimiter` instances when `multiLimiter` is instantiated, we can simply return the most restrictive limit, which will be the first element in the slice.

The `Wait` method loops through all the child rate limiters and calls `Wait` on each of them. These calls may or may not block, but we need to notify each rate limiter of the request so we can decrement our token bucket. By waiting for each limiter, we are guaranteed to wait for exactly the time of the longest wait. This is because if we perform smaller waits that only wait for segments of the longest wait and then hit the longest wait, the longest wait will be recalculated to only be the remaining time. This is because while the earlier waits were blocking, the latter waits were refilling their buckets; any waits after will be returned instantaneously.

Now that we have the means to express rate limits from multiple rate limits, let's take the opportunity to do so. Let's redefine our `APIConnection` to have limits both per second and per minute:

```
    func Open() *APIConnection {
        secondLimit := rate.NewLimiter(Per(2, time.Second), 1)  ❶
        minuteLimit := rate.NewLimiter(Per(10, time.Minute), 10)  ❷
        return &APIConnection{
            rateLimiter: MultiLimiter(secondLimit, minuteLimit),  ❸
        }
    }
```

```
type APIConnection struct {
    rateLimiter RateLimiter
}

func (a *APIConnection) ReadFile(ctx context.Context) error {
    if err := a.rateLimiter.Wait(ctx); err != nil {
        return err
    }
    // Pretend we do work here
    return nil
}

func (a *APIConnection) ResolveAddress(ctx context.Context) error {
    if err := a.rateLimiter.Wait(ctx); err != nil {
        return err
    }
    // Pretend we do work here
    return nil
}
```

❶ Here we define our limit per second with no burstiness.

❷ Here we define our limit per minute with a burstiness of 10 to give the users their initial pool. The limit per second will ensure we don't overload our system with requests.

❸ We then combine the two limits and set this as the master rate limiter for our `APIConnection`.

Running this code produces:

```
22:46:10 ResolveAddress
22:46:10 ReadFile
22:46:11 ReadFile
22:46:11 ReadFile
22:46:12 ReadFile
22:46:12 ReadFile
22:46:13 ReadFile
22:46:13 ReadFile
22:46:14 ReadFile
22:46:14 ReadFile
22:46:16 ResolveAddress
22:46:22 ResolveAddress
22:46:28 ReadFile
22:46:34 ResolveAddress
22:46:40 ResolveAddress
22:46:46 ResolveAddress
22:46:52 ResolveAddress
22:46:58 ResolveAddress
22:47:04 ResolveAddress
```

```
22:47:10 ResolveAddress
22:47:10 Done.
```

As you can see we make two requests per second up until request #11, at which point we begin making requests every six seconds. This is because we drained our available pool of per-minute request tokens, and become limited by this cap.

It might be slightly counterintuitive why request #11 occurs after only two seconds rather than six like the rest of the requests. Remember that although we limit our API requests to 10 a minute, that minute is a sliding window of time. By the time we reach the eleventh request, our per-minute rate limiter has accrued another token.

Defining limits like this allows us to express our coarse-grained limits plainly while still limiting the number of requests at a finer level of detail.

This technique also allows us to begin thinking across dimensions other than time. When you rate limit a system, you're probably going to limit more than one thing. You'll likely have some kind of limit on the number of API requests, but in addition, you'll probably also have limits on other resources like disk access, network access, etc. Let's flesh out our example a bit and set up rate limits for disk and network:

```go
func Open() *APIConnection {
    return &APIConnection{
        apiLimit: MultiLimiter( ❶
            rate.NewLimiter(Per(2, time.Second), 2),
            rate.NewLimiter(Per(10, time.Minute), 10),
        ),
        diskLimit: MultiLimiter( ❷
            rate.NewLimiter(rate.Limit(1), 1),
        ),
        networkLimit: MultiLimiter( ❸
            rate.NewLimiter(Per(3, time.Second), 3),
        ),
    }
}

type APIConnection struct {
    networkLimit,
    diskLimit,
    apiLimit RateLimiter
}

func (a *APIConnection) ReadFile(ctx context.Context) error {
    err := MultiLimiter(a.apiLimit, a.diskLimit).Wait(ctx) ❹
    if err != nil {
        return err
    }
    // Pretend we do work here
    return nil
}
```

```
func (a *APIConnection) ResolveAddress(ctx context.Context) error {
    err := MultiLimiter(a.apiLimit, a.networkLimit).Wait(ctx)  ❺
    if err != nil {
        return err
    }
    // Pretend we do work here
    return nil
}
```

❶ Here we set up a rate limiter for API calls. There are limits for both requests per second and requests per minute.

❷ Here we set up a rate limiter for disk reads. We'll only limit this to one read per second.

❸ For networking, we'll set up a limit of three requests per second.

❹ When we go to read a file, we'll combine the limits from the API limiter and the disk limiter.

❺ When we require network access, we'll combine the limits from the API limiter and the network limiter.

Running this code produces:

```
01:40:15 ResolveAddress
01:40:15 ReadFile
01:40:16 ReadFile
01:40:17 ResolveAddress
01:40:17 ResolveAddress
01:40:17 ReadFile
01:40:18 ResolveAddress
01:40:18 ResolveAddress
01:40:19 ResolveAddress
01:40:19 ResolveAddress
01:40:21 ResolveAddress
01:40:27 ResolveAddress
01:40:33 ResolveAddress
01:40:39 ReadFile
01:40:45 ReadFile
01:40:51 ReadFile
01:40:57 ReadFile
01:41:03 ReadFile
01:41:09 ReadFile
01:41:15 ReadFile
01:41:15 Done.
```

I could build another time table here to break down why each call is happening where, but that would miss the point. Instead, let's focus on the fact that we're able to compose logical rate limiters into groups that make sense for each call, and the

`APIClient` does the correct thing. If we wanted to make a casual observation about how it's working, we could note that the API calls involving network access appear to happen with more regularity and finish in the first two-thirds of calls. This may have to do with when the goroutines are scheduled, but it's much more likely that our rate limiters are doing their jobs!

I should also mention that the `rate.Limiter` type has a few other tricks up its sleeve for optimizations and different use cases. I have only discussed its ability to wait until the token bucket receives another token, but if you're interested in using it, just know that it has a few other capabilities.

In this section, we've looked at the justification for utilizing rate limits, an algorithm for building one, a Go implementation of the token bucket algorithm, and how to compose token bucket limiters into larger, more complex rate limiters. This should give you a good overview of rate limits, and help you get started using them in the field.

Healing Unhealthy Goroutines

In long-lived processes such as daemons, it's very common to have a set of long-lived goroutines. These goroutines are usually blocked, waiting on data to come to them through some means, so that they can wake up, do their work, and then pass the data on. Sometimes the goroutines are dependent on a resource that you don't have very good control of. Maybe a goroutine receives a request to pull data from a web service, or maybe it's monitoring an ephemeral file. The point is that it can be very easy for a goroutine to become stuck in a bad state from which it cannot recover without external help. If you separate your concerns, you might even say that it shouldn't be the concern of a goroutine doing work to know how to heal itself from a bad state. In a long-running process, it can be useful to create a mechanism that ensures your goroutines remain healthy and restarts them if they become unhealthy. We'll refer to this process of restarting goroutines as "healing."[2]

To heal goroutines, we'll use our heartbeat pattern to check up on the liveliness of the goroutine we're monitoring. The type of heartbeat will be determined by what you're trying to monitor, but if your goroutine can become livelocked, make sure that the heartbeat contains some kind of information indicating that the goroutine is not only up, but doing useful work. In this section, for simplicity, we'll only consider whether goroutines are live or dead.

We'll call the logic that monitors a goroutine's health a *steward*, and the goroutine that it monitors a *ward*. Stewards will also be responsible for restarting a ward's goroutine

---

2 Those of you familiar with erlang may recognize this concept! Erlang's supervisors do much the same thing.

should it become unhealthy. To do so, it will need a reference to a function that can start the goroutine. Let's see what a steward might look like:

```
type startGoroutineFn func(
    done <-chan interface{},
    pulseInterval time.Duration,
) (heartbeat <-chan interface{}) ❶

newSteward := func(
    timeout time.Duration,
    startGoroutine startGoroutineFn,
) startGoroutineFn { ❷
    return func(
        done <-chan interface{},
        pulseInterval time.Duration,
    ) (<-chan interface{}) {
        heartbeat := make(chan interface{})
        go func() {
            defer close(heartbeat)

            var wardDone chan interface{}
            var wardHeartbeat <-chan interface{}
            startWard := func() { ❸
                wardDone = make(chan interface{}) ❹
                wardHeartbeat = startGoroutine(or(wardDone, done), timeout/2) ❺
            }
            startWard()
            pulse := time.Tick(pulseInterval)

        monitorLoop:
            for {
                timeoutSignal := time.After(timeout)

                for { ❻
                    select {
                    case <-pulse:
                        select {
                        case heartbeat <- struct{}{}:
                        default:
                        }
                    case <-wardHeartbeat: ❼
                        continue monitorLoop
                    case <-timeoutSignal: ❽
                        log.Println("steward: ward unhealthy; restarting")
                        close(wardDone)
                        startWard()
                        continue monitorLoop
                    case <-done:
                        return
                    }
                }
            }
        }
```

```
        }()

        return heartbeat
    }
}
```

❶ Here we define the signature of a goroutine that can be monitored and restarted. We see the familiar done channel, and pulseInterval and heartbeat from the heartbeat pattern.

❷ On this line we see that a steward takes in a timeout for the goroutine it will be monitoring, and a function, startGoroutine, to start the goroutine it's monitoring. Interestingly, the steward itself returns a startGoroutineFn indicating that the steward itself is also monitorable.

❸ Here we define a closure that encodes a consistent way to start the goroutine we're monitoring.

❹ This is where we create a new channel that we'll pass into the ward goroutine in case we need to signal that it should halt.

❺ Here we start the goroutine we'll be monitoring. We want the ward goroutine to halt if either the steward is halted, or the steward wants to halt the ward goroutine, so we wrap both done channels in a logical-or. The pulseInterval we pass in is half of the timeout period, although as we discussed in "Heartbeats" on page 161, this can be tweaked.

❻ This is our inner loop, which ensures that the steward can send out pulses of its own.

❼ Here we see that if we receive the ward's pulse, we continue our monitoring loop.

❽ This line indicates that if we don't receive a pulse from the ward within our timeout period, we request that the ward halt and we begin a new ward goroutine. We then continue monitoring.

Our for loop is a *little* busy, but as long as you're familiar with the patterns involved, it's relatively straightforward to read through. Let's give our steward a test run. What happens if we monitor a goroutine that is misbehaving? Let's take a look:

```
log.SetOutput(os.Stdout)
log.SetFlags(log.Ltime | log.LUTC)

doWork := func(done <-chan interface{}, _ time.Duration) <-chan interface{} {
    log.Println("ward: Hello, I'm irresponsible!")
    go func() {
```

```
        <-done ❶
        log.Println("ward: I am halting.")
    }()
    return nil
}
doWorkWithSteward := newSteward(4*time.Second, doWork) ❷

done := make(chan interface{})
time.AfterFunc(9*time.Second, func() { ❸
    log.Println("main: halting steward and ward.")
    close(done)
})

for range doWorkWithSteward(done, 4*time.Second) {} ❹
log.Println("Done")
```

❶ Here we see that this goroutine isn't doing anything but waiting to be canceled.
    It's also not sending out any pulses.

❷ This line creates a function that will create a steward for the goroutine doWork
    starts. We set the timeout for doWork at four seconds.

❸ Here we halt the steward and its ward after nine seconds so that our example will
    end.

❹ Finally, we start the steward and range over its pulses to prevent our example
    from halting.

This example produces the following output:

```
18:28:07 ward: Hello, I'm irresponsible!
18:28:11 steward: ward unhealthy; restarting
18:28:11 ward: Hello, I'm irresponsible!
18:28:11 ward: I am halting.
18:28:15 steward: ward unhealthy; restarting
18:28:15 ward: Hello, I'm irresponsible!
18:28:15 ward: I am halting.
18:28:16 main: halting steward and ward.
18:28:16 ward: I am halting.
18:28:16 Done
```

It looks like this is working quite nicely! Our ward is a little simplistic though: other
than what's necessary for cancellation and heartbeats, it takes in no parameters and
returns no arguments. How might we create a ward that has a shape that can be used
with our steward? We could rewrite or generate the steward to fit our wards each
time, but this is both cumbersome and unnecessary; instead, we'll use closures. Let's
take a look at a ward that will generate an integer stream based on a discrete list of
values:

```
doWorkFn := func(
    done <-chan interface{},
    intList ...int,
) (startGoroutineFn, <-chan interface{}) { ❶
    intChanStream := make(chan (<-chan interface{})) ❷
    intStream := bridge(done, intChanStream)
    doWork := func(
        done <-chan interface{},
        pulseInterval time.Duration,
    ) <-chan interface{} { ❸
        intStream := make(chan interface{}) ❹
        heartbeat := make(chan interface{})
        go func() {
            defer close(intStream)
            select {
            case intChanStream <- intStream: ❺
            case <-done:
                return
            }

            pulse := time.Tick(pulseInterval)

            for {
                valueLoop:
                for _, intVal := range intList {
                    if intVal < 0 {
                        log.Printf("negative value: %v\n", intVal) ❻
                        return
                    }

                    for {
                        select {
                        case <-pulse:
                            select {
                            case heartbeat <- struct{}{}:
                            default:
                            }
                        case intStream <- intVal:
                            continue valueLoop
                        case <-done:
                            return
                        }
                    }
                }
            }
        }()
        return heartbeat
    }
    return doWork, intStream
}
```

❶ Here we'll take in the values we want our ward to close over, and return any channels our ward will be using to communicate back on.

❷ This line creates our channel of channels as part of the bridge pattern.

❸ Here we create the closure that will be started and monitored by our steward.

❹ This is where we instantiate the channel we'll communicate on within this instance of our ward's goroutine.

❺ Here we let the bridge know about the new channel we'll be communicating on.

❻ This line simulates an unhealthy ward by logging an error when we encounter a negative number and returning from the goroutine.

You can see that since we'll potentially be starting multiple copies of our ward, we make use of bridge channels (see "The bridge-channel" on page 122) to help present a single uninterrupted channel to the consumer of doWork. Using these techniques, our wards can become arbitrarily complex simply by composing patterns. Let's see how utilizing this feels:

```
log.SetFlags(log.Ltime | log.LUTC)
log.SetOutput(os.Stdout)

done := make(chan interface{})
defer close(done)

doWork, intStream := doWorkFn(done, 1, 2, -1, 3, 4, 5) ❶
doWorkWithSteward := newSteward(1*time.Millisecond, doWork) ❷
doWorkWithSteward(done, 1*time.Hour) ❸

for intVal := range take(done, intStream, 6) { ❹
    fmt.Printf("Received: %v\n", intVal)
}
```

❶ This line creates our ward's function, allowing it to close over our variadic slice of integers, and return a stream that it will communicate back on.

❷ Here we create our steward that will monitor the doWork closure. Because we expect failures fairly quickly, we'll set the monitoring period at just one millisecond.

❸ Here we tell the steward to start the ward and begin monitoring.

❹ Finally, we use one of the pipeline stages we developed and take the first six values from our intStream.

Running this code produces:

```
Received: 1
23:25:33 negative value: -1
Received: 2
23:25:33 steward: ward unhealthy; restarting
Received: 1
23:25:33 negative value: -1
Received: 2
23:25:33 steward: ward unhealthy; restarting
Received: 1
23:25:33 negative value: -1
Received: 2
```

Interspersed with the values we receive, we see errors from the ward, and our steward detecting them and restarting the ward. You might also notice that we only ever receive values 1 and 2. This is a symptom of our ward starting from scratch every time. When developing your wards, if your system is sensitive to duplicate values, be sure to take that into account. You might also consider writing a steward that exits after a certain number of failures. In this case, we could have simply made our generator stateful by updating the intList we are closed over in every iteration. Whereas before we had this:

```
valueLoop:
for _, intVal := range intList {
    // ...
}
```

We could instead write this:

```
valueLoop:
    for {
        intVal := intList[0]
        intList = intList[1:]
        // ...
    }
```

This would save our place between our ward's restarts, although we would remain stuck at our invalid negative number, and our ward would continue to fail.

Using this pattern can help ensure your long-lived goroutines stay up and healthy.

Summary

In this chapter, we've covered some ways to keep your systems stable and understandable as the problem domains they take on necessitate larger systems that are perhaps distributed. This chapter also demonstrated how Go's concurrency primitives scale as you create higher-order abstractions. Without the benefit of a language designed around concurrency, these patterns would likely be much more cumbersome, and much less robust.

In the final chapter, we're going to explore the internals of some of Go's runtime to help you develop a deep understanding of how things work. We'll also explore some useful tools that will make the job of developing and debugging Go software a bit easier.

CHAPTER 6

Goroutines and the Go Runtime

When working in Go, it's fun to dive right into utilizing concurrency because the language just makes it so easy! Very rarely have I needed to understand how the runtime stitches everything together under the covers. Still, there *have* been times when this information has been useful, and all of the things discussed in Chapter 2 are made possible by the runtime, so it's worth taking a moment to take a peek at how the runtime works. It has the added benefit of being interesting!

Of all the things the Go runtime does for you, spawning and managing goroutines is probably the most beneficial to you and your software. Google, the company that birthed Go, has a history of putting computer science theories and white papers to work, so it's not surprising that Go contains several ideas from academia. What is surprising is the amount of sophistication behind each goroutine. Go has done a wonderful job of wielding some powerful ideas that make your program more performant, but abstracting away these details and presenting a very simple facade for developers to work with.

Work Stealing

As we discussed in the sections "How This Helps You" on page 29 and "Goroutines" on page 37, Go will handle multiplexing goroutines onto OS threads for you. The algorithm it uses to do this is known as a *work stealing* strategy. What does that mean?

First, let's look at a naive strategy for sharing work across many processors, something called *fair scheduling*. In an effort to ensure all processors were equally utilized, we could evenly distribute the load between all available processors. Imagine there are n processors and x tasks to perform. In the fair scheduling strategy, each processor would get x/n tasks:

```
<Schedule Task 1>
<Schedule Task 2>
<Schedule Task 3>
<Schedule Task 4>
```

Unfortunately, there are problems with this approach. If you remember from the section "Goroutines" on page 37, Go models concurrency using a fork-join model. In a fork-join paradigm, tasks are likely dependent on one another, and it turns out naively splitting them among processors will likely cause one of the processors to be underutilized. Not only that, but it can also lead to poor cache locality as tasks that require the same data are scheduled on other processors. Let's take a look at an example of why.

Consider a simple program that results in the work distribution outlined previously. What would happen if task two took longer to complete than tasks one and three combined?

Time	P1	P2
	T1	T2
n+a	T3	T2
n+a+b	(idle)	T4

Whatever the duration of time between a and b, processor one will be idle.

What happens if there are interdepencies between tasks—if a task allocated to one processor requires the result from a task allocated to another processor? For example, what if task one was dependent on task four?

Time	P1	P2
	T1	T2
n+a	(blocked)	T2
n+a+b	(blocked)	T4
n+a+b+c	T1	(idle)
n+a+b+c+d	T3	(idle)

In this scenario, processor one is completely idle while tasks two and four are being computed. While processor one was blocked on task one, and processor two was occupied with task two, processor one could have been working on task four to unblock itself.

OK, these sound like basic load-balancing problems that maybe a FIFO queue can help with, so let's try that: work tasks get scheduled into the queue, and our processors dequeue tasks as they have capacity, or block on joins. This is the first type of work stealing algorithm we'll look at. Does this solve the problem?

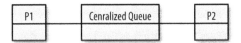

The answer is *maybe*. It's better than simply dividing the tasks among the processors because it solves the problem with underutilized processors, but we've now introduced a centralized data structure that all the processors must use. As discussed in "Memory Access Synchronization" on page 8, we know that continually entering and exiting critical sections is extremely costly. Not only that, but our cache locality problems have only been exacerbated: we're now going to load the centralized queue into each processor's cache every time it wants to enqueue or dequeue a task. Still, for coarse-grained operations, this can be a valid approach. However, goroutines usually aren't coarse-grained, so a centralized queue probably isn't a great choice for our work scheduling algorithm.

The next leap we could make is to decentralize the work queues. We could give each processor its own thread and a double-ended queue, or *deque*, like this:

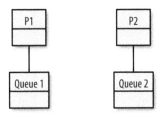

OK, we've solved our problem with a central data structure under high contention, but what about the problems with cache locality and processor utilization? And on that topic, if the work begins on P1, and all forked tasks are placed on P1's queue, how does work ever make it to P2? And don't we have a problem with context switching now that tasks are moving between queues? Let's go through the rules of how a work-stealing algorithm operates with distributed queues.

As a refresher, remember that Go follows a fork-join model for concurrency. Forks are when goroutines are started, and join points are when two or more goroutines are synchronized through channels or types in the sync package. The work stealing algorithm follows a few basic rules. Given a thread of execution:

1. At a fork point, add tasks to the tail of the deque associated with the thread.
2. If the thread is idle, steal work from the head of deque associated with some other random thread.
3. At a join point that cannot be realized yet (i.e., the goroutine it is synchronized with has not completed yet), pop work off the tail of the thread's own deque.
4. If the thread's deque is empty, either:
   a. Stall at a join.
   b. Steal work from the head of a random thread's associated deque.

This is a bit abstract, so let's look at some real code and see this algorithm in action. Take the following program, which computes the Fibonacci sequence recursively:

```
var fib func(n int) <-chan int
fib = func(n int) <-chan int {
    result := make(chan int)
    go func() {
        defer close(result)
        if n <= 2 {
            result <- 1
            return
        }
        result <- <-fib(n-1) + <-fib(n-2)
    }()
    return result
}

fmt.Printf("fib(4) = %d", <-fib(4))
```

Let's see how this version of a work-stealing algorithm would operate in this Go program. Let's say this program is executing on a hypothetical machine with two single-core processors. We'll spawn one OS thread on each processor, T1 for processor one, and T2 for processor two. As we walk through this example, I'll flip from T1 to T2 in an effort to provide some structure. In reality, none of this is deterministic.

So our program begins. Initially, we just have one goroutine, the *main goroutine*, and we'll assume it's scheduled on processor one:

T1 call stack	T1 work deque	T2 call stack	T2 work deque
(main goroutine)			

Next, we reach the call to fib(4). This goroutine will get scheduled and placed onto the tail of T1's work deque, and the parent goroutine will continue processing:

T1 call stack	T1 work deque	T2 call stack	T2 work deque
(main goroutine)	fib(4)		

At this point, depending on the timing, one of two things will happen: either T1 or T2 will steal the goroutine that hosts the call to fib(4). For this example, to more clearly illustrate the algorithm, we'll assume T1 wins the steal; however, it's important to note that either thread could win.

T1 call stack	T1 work deque	T2 call stack	T2 work deque
(main goroutine) (unrealized join point)			
fib(4)			

fib(4) runs on T1 and—because the order of operations for addition is left-to-right —pushes fib(3) and then fib(2) onto the tail of its deque:

T1 call stack	T1 work deque	T2 call stack	T2 work deque
(main goroutine) (unrealized join point)	fib(3)		
fib(4)	fib(2)		

At this point, T2 is still idle, so it plucks fib(3) from the head of T1's deque. Notice here that fib(2)—the last thing fib(4) pushed onto the queue, and therefore the first thing T1 will most likely need to calculate—remains on T1. We'll discuss why this is important later.

T1 call stack	T1 work deque	T2 call stack	T2 work deque
(main goroutine) (unrealized join point)	fib(2)	fib(3)	
fib(4)			

Meanwhile, T1 reaches a point where it cannot continue working on fib(4) because it's waiting on the channels returned from fib(3) and fib(2). This is the *unrealized join point* in step three of our algorithm. Because of this, it pops work off the tail of its own queue, here fib(2):

T1 call stack	T1 work deque	T2 call stack	T2 work deque
(main goroutine) (unrealized join point)		fib(3)	
fib(4) (unrealized join point)			
fib(2)			

It gets a little confusing here. Because we're not utilizing backtracking in our recursive algorithm, we're going to schedule another goroutine to calculate `fib(2)`. This is a new and separate goroutine from the one that was just scheduled on T1. The one that was just scheduled on T1 was part of the call to `fib(4)` (i.e., 4-2); the new goroutine is part of the call to `fib(3)` (i.e., 3-1). Here are the newly scheduled goroutines from the call to `fib(3)`:

T1 call stack	T1 work deque	T2 call stack	T2 work deque
(main goroutine) (unrealized join point)		`fib(3)`	`fib(2)`
`fib(4)` (unrealized join point)			`fib(1)`
`fib(2)`			

Next, T1 reaches the base case of our recursive Fibonacci algorithm (n <= 2) and returns 1:

T1 call stack	T1 work deque	T2 call stack	T2 work deque
(main goroutine) (unrealized join point)		`fib(3)`	`fib(2)`
`fib(4)` (unrealized join point)			`fib(1)`
(returns 1)			

Then T2 reaches an unrealized join point and pops work off the tail of its deque:

T1 call stack	T1 work deque	T2 call stack	T2 work deque
(main goroutine) (unrealized join point)		`fib(3)` (unrealized join point)	`fib(2)`
`fib(4)` (unrealized join point)		`fib(1)`	
(returns 1)			

Now T1 is once again idle so it steals work from the head of T2's work deque:

T1 call stack	T1 work deque	T2 call stack	T2 work deque
(main goroutine) (unrealized join point)		`fib(3)` (unrealized join point)	
`fib(4)` (unrealized join point)		`fib(1)`	
`fib(2)`			

T2 then reaches the base case once again (n <= 2) and returns 1:

T1 call stack	T1 work deque	T2 call stack	T2 work deque
(main goroutine) (unrealized join point)		fib(3) (unrealized join point)	
fib(4) (unrealized join point)		(returns 1)	
fib(2)			

Next, T1 also reaches the base case and returns 1:

T1 call stack	T1 work deque	T2 call stack	T2 work deque
(main goroutine) (unrealized join point)		fib(3) (unrealized join point)	
fib(4) (unrealized join point)		(returns 1)	
(returns 1)			

T2's call to fib(3) now has two *realized join points*; that is, the calls to both fib(2) and fib(1) have returned results on their channels, and the two goroutines spawned have joined back to their parent goroutine—the one hosting the call to fib(3). It performs its addition (1+1=2) and returns the result on its channel:

T1 call stack	T1 work deque	T2 call stack	T2 work deque
(main goroutine) (unrealized join point)		(returns 2)	
fib(4) (unrealized join point)			

The same thing then happens again: the goroutine hosting the call to fib(4) had two unrealized join points: fib(3) and fib(2). We just completed the join for fib(3) in the previous step, and the join to fib(2) was completed as the last task T2 completed. Once again, the addition is performed (2+1=3) and the result is returned on fib(4)'s channel:

T1 call stack	T1 work deque	T2 call stack	T2 work deque
(main goroutine) (unrealized join point)			
(return 3)			

At this point, we have realized the join point in the main goroutine (`<-fib(4)`), and the main goroutine can continue. It does so by printing the result:

T1 call stack	T1 work deque	T2 call stack	T2 work deque
(print 3)			

Now, let's examine some interesting properties of this algorithm. Recall that a thread of execution both pushes and (when necessary) pops from the tail of its work deque. The work sitting on the tail of its deque has a couple of interesting properties:

It's the work most likely needed to complete the parent's join.
Completing joins more quickly means our program is likely to perform better, and also keep fewer things in memory.

It's the work most likely to still be in our processor's cache.
Since it's the work the thread was last working on prior to its current work, it's likely that this information remains in the cache of the CPU the thread is executing on. This means fewer cache misses!

Overall, scheduling work in this manner has many implicit performance benefits.

Stealing Tasks or Continuations?

One thing we've kind of glossed over is the question of what work we are enqueuing and stealing. Under a fork-join paradigm, there are two options: tasks and continuations. To make sure that you have a clear understanding of what tasks and continuations are in Go, let's look at our Fibonacci program once again:

```
var fib func(n int) <-chan int
fib = func(n int) <-chan int {
    result := make(chan int)
    go func() { ❶
        defer close(result)
        if n <= 2 {
            result <- 1
            return
        }
        result <- <-fib(n-1) + <-fib(n-2)
    }()
    return result ❷
}

fmt.Printf("fib(4) = %d", <-fib(4))
```

❶ In Go, goroutines are tasks.

❷ Everything after a goroutine is called is the continuation.

In our previous walkthrough of a distributed-queue work-stealing algorithm, we were enqueuing tasks, or goroutines. Since a goroutine hosts functions that nicely encapsulate a body of work, this is a natural way to think about things; however, this is not actually how Go's work-stealing algorithm works. Go's work-stealing algorithm enqueues and steals continuations.

So why does this matter? What does enqueing and stealing continuations do for us that enqueing and stealing tasks does not? To begin answering this question, let's look at our join points.

Under our algorithm, when a thread of execution reaches an unrealized join point, the thread must pause execution and go fishing for a task to steal. This is called a *stalling join* because it is stalling at the join while looking for work to do. Both task-stealing and continuation-stealing algorithms have stalling joins, but there is a significant difference in how often stalls occur.

Consider this: when creating a goroutine, it is very likely that your program will want the function in that goroutine to execute. It is also reasonably likely that the continuation from that goroutine will at some point want to join with that goroutine. And it's not uncommon for the continuation to attempt a join before the goroutine has finished completing. Given these axioms, when scheduling a goroutine, it makes sense to immediately begin working on it.

Now think back to the properties of a thread pushing and popping work to/from the tail of its deque, and other threads popping work from the head. If we push the continuation onto the tail of the deque, it's least likely to get stolen by another thread that is popping things from the head of the deque, and therefore it becomes very likely that we'll be able to just pick it back up when we're finished executing our goroutine, thus avoiding a stall. This also makes the forked task look a lot like a function call: the thread jumps to executing the goroutine and then returns to the continuation after it's finished.

Let's look at applying continuation-stealing to our Fibonacci program. Since representing continuations is a bit less clear than tasks, we'll use the following conventions:

- When a continuation is enqueued on a work deque, we'll list it as cont. of X.
- When a continuation is dequeued for execution, we'll implicitly convert the continuation to the next invocation of fib.

What follows is a closer representation of what Go's runtime is doing.

Once again we start out with the main goroutine:

T1 call stack	T1 work deque	T2 call stack	T2 work deque
main			

The main goroutine calls `fib(4)` and the continuation from this call is enqueued onto the tail of T1's work deque:

T1 call stack	T1 work deque	T2 call stack	T2 work deque
fib(4)	cont. of main		

T2 is idle so it steals the continuation of main:

T1 call stack	T1 work deque	T2 call stack	T2 work deque
fib(4)		cont. of main	

The call to `fib(4)` then schedules `fib(3)`, which is immediately executed, and T1 pushes the continuation of `fib(4)` onto the tail of its deque:

T1 call stack	T1 work deque	T2 call stack	T2 work deque
fib(3)	cont. of fib(4)	cont. of main	

When T2 attempts to execute the continuation of main, it reaches an unrealized join point; therefore, it steals more work from T1. This time, it's the continuation of the call to `fib(4)`:

T1 call stack	T1 work deque	T2 call stack	T2 work deque
fib(3)		cont. of main (unrealized join point)	
		cont. of fib(4)	

Next, T1's call to `fib(3)` schedules the goroutine for `fib(2)` and immediately begins executing it. The continuation of `fib(3)` is pushed onto the tail of its work deque:

T1 call stack	T1 work deque	T2 call stack	T2 work deque
fib(2)	cont. of fib(3)	cont. of main	
		cont. of fib(4)	

T2's execution of the continuation of `fib(4)` picks up where T1 left off, and it schedules `fib(2)`, begins executing it immediately, and once again enqueues `fib(4)`:

T1 call stack	T1 work deque	T2 call stack	T2 work deque
fib(2)	cont. of fib(3)	cont. of main (unrealized join point)	cont. of fib(4)
		fib(2)	

Next, T1's call to `fib(2)` reaches the base case of our recursive algorithm and returns 1:

T1 call stack	T1 work deque	T2 call stack	T2 work deque
(returns 1)	cont. of `fib(3)`	cont. of main (unrealized join point)	cont. of `fib(4)`
		`fib(2)`	

Then T2 also reaches the base case and returns 1:

T1 call stack	T1 work deque	T2 call stack	T2 work deque
(returns 1)	cont. of `fib(3)`	cont. of main (unrealized join point)	cont. of `fib(4)`
		(returns 1)	

T1 then steals work from its own queue and begins executing `fib(1)`. Notice how the call chain on T1 was: `fib(3)` → `fib(2)` → `fib(1)`. This is the benefit of continuation stealing we discussed earlier!

T1 call stack	T1 work deque	T2 call stack	T2 work deque
`fib(1)`		cont. of main (unrealized join point)	cont. of `fib(4)`
		(returns 1)	

T2 is then at the end of the continuation of `fib(4)`, but only one join point has been realized: `fib(2)`. The call to `fib(3)` is still being processed by T1. T2 idles since there is no work to steal:

T1 call stack	T1 work deque	T2 call stack	T2 work deque
`fib(1)`		cont. of main (unrealized join point)	
		`fib(4)` (unrealized join point)	

T1 is now at the end of its continuation, `fib(3)`, and both of its join points from `fib(2)` and `fib(1)` have been satisfied. T1 returns 2:

T1 call stack	T1 work deque	T2 call stack	T2 work deque
(returns 2)		cont. of main (unrealized join point)	
		(returns 2)	

Now both of the join points for fib(4), fib(3), and fib(2) have been satisfied. T2 is able to perform its computation and return the results (2+1=3):

T1 call stack	T1 work deque	T2 call stack		T2 work deque
		cont. of main (unrealized join point)		
		(returns 3)		

Finally, the main goroutine's join point has been realized and it receives the value from the call to fib(4) and is able to print the result, 3:

T1 call stack	T1 work deque	T2 call stack	T2 work deque
		main (prints 3)	

When we walked through this, we briefly saw how continuations helped execute things serially on T1. If we look at the stats of this run (with continuation stealing) versus the run with task stealing, a clearer picture of the benefits begins to emerge:

Statistic	Continuation stealing	Task stealing
# Steps	14	15
Max Deque Length	2	2
# Stalled Joins	2 (all on idle threads)	3 (all on busy threads)
Size of call stack	2	3

These statistics may seem like they're close, but if we extrapolate to larger programs we can begin to see how continuation stealing could provide a significant benefit.

Let's also take a look at what running this looks like with only one thread of execution:

T1 call stack	T1 work deque
main	

T1 call stack	T1 work deque
fib(4)	main

T1 call stack	T1 work deque
fib(3)	main
	cont. of fib(4)

T1 call stack	T1 work deque
fib(2)	main
	cont. of fib(4)
	cont. of fib(3)

T1 call stack	T1 work deque
(returns 1)	main
	cont. of fib(4)
	cont. of fib(3)

T1 call stack	T1 work deque
fib(1)	main
	cont. of fib(4)

T1 call stack	T1 work deque
(returns 1)	main
	cont. of fib(4)

T1 call stack	T1 work deque
(returns 2)	main
	cont. of fib(4)

T1 call stack	T1 work deque
fib(2)	main

T1 call stack	T1 work deque
(return 1)	main

T1 call stack	T1 work deque
(return 3)	main

T1 call stack	T1 work deque
main (print 3)	

Interesting! The runtime on a single thread using goroutines is the same as if we had just used functions! This is another benefit of continuation stealing.

All things considered, stealing continuations are considered to be theoretically superior to stealing tasks, and therefore it is best to queue the continuation and not the goroutine. As you can see from the following table, stealing continuations has several benefits:

	Continuation	Child
Queue Size	Bounded	Unbounded
Order of Execution	Serial	Out of Order
Join Point	Nonstalling	Stalling

So why don't all work-stealing algorithms implement continuation stealing? Well, continuation stealing usually requires support from the compiler. Luckily, Go has its own compiler, and continuation stealing is how Go's work-stealing algorithm is implemented. Languages that don't have this luxury usually implement task, or so-called "child," stealing as a library.

While this model is closer to Go's algorithm, it still doesn't represent the entire picture. Go performs additional optimizations. Before we analyze those, let's set the stage by starting to use the Go scheduler's nomenclature as laid out in the source code.

Go's scheduler has three main concepts:

G

A goroutine.

M

An OS thread (also referenced as a machine in the source code).

P

A context (also referenced as a processor in the source code).

In our discussion about work stealing, *M* is equivalent to *T*, and *P* is equivalent to the work deque (changing GOMAXPROCS changes how many of these are allocated). The *G* is a goroutine, but keep in mind it represents the current *state* of a goroutine, most notably its program counter (PC). This allows a G to represent a continuation so Go can do continuation stealing.

In Go's runtime, Ms are started, which then host Ps, which then schedule and host Gs:

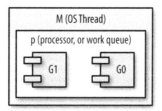

Personally, I find it difficult to follow analysis of how this algorithm works when only this notation is used, so I'll be using their full names in this analysis. Alright, now that we have our terms down, let's take a look at how Go's scheduler works!

As we mentioned, the GOMAXPROCS setting controls how many contexts are available for use by the runtime. The default setting is for there to be one context per logical CPU on the host machine. Unlike contexts, there may be more or less OS threads than cores to help Go's runtime manage things like garbage collection and goroutines. I bring this up because there is one very important guarantee in the runtime: there will always be at least enough OS threads available to handle hosting every context. This allows the runtime to make an important optimization. The runtime also contains a thread pool for threads that aren't currently being utilized. Now let's talk about those optimizations!

Consider what would happen if any of the goroutines were blocked either by input/output or by making a system call outside of Go's runtime. The OS thread that hosts the goroutine would also be blocked and would be unable to make progress or host any other goroutines. Logically, this is just fine, but from a performance perspective, Go could do more to keep processors on the machine as active as possible.

What Go does in this situation is dissociate the context from the OS thread so that the context can be handed off to another, unblocked, OS thread. This allows the context to schedule further goroutines, which allows the runtime to keep the host machine's CPUs active. The blocked goroutine remains associated with the blocked thread.

When the goroutine eventually becomes unblocked, the host OS thread attempts to steal back a context from one of the other OS threads so that it can continue executing the previously blocked goroutine. However, sometimes this is not always possible. In this case, the thread will place its goroutine on a *global* context, the thread will go to sleep, and it will be put into the runtime's thread pool for future use (for instance, if a goroutine becomes blocked again).

The global context we just mentioned doesn't fit into our prior discussions of abstract work-stealing algorithms. It's an implementation detail that is necessitated by how Go is optimizing CPU utilization. To ensure that goroutines placed into the global context aren't there perpetually, a few extra steps are added into the work-stealing algorithm. Periodically, a context will check the global context to see if there are any goroutines there, and when a context's queue is empty, it will first check the global context for work to steal before checking other OS threads' contexts.

Other than input/output and system calls, Go also allows goroutines to be preempted during any function call. This works in tandem with Go's philosophy of preferring very fine-grained concurrent tasks by ensuring the runtime can efficiently schedule work. One notable exception that the team has been trying to solve (*https:// github.com/golang/go/issues/10958*) is goroutines that perform no input/output, system calls, or function calls. Currently, these kinds of goroutines are not preemptable and can cause significant issues like long GC waits, or even deadlocks. Fortunately, from an anecdotal perspective, this is a vanishingly small occurrence.

Presenting All of This to the Developer

Now that you understand how goroutines work under the covers, let's once again pull back and reiterate how developers interface with all of this: the go keyword. That's it!

Slap the word go before a function or closure, and you've automatically scheduled a task that will be run in the most efficient way for the machine it's running on. As developers, we're still thinking in the primitives we're familiar with: functions. We don't have to understand a new way of doing things, complicated data structures, or scheduling algorithms.

Scaling, efficiency, and simplicity. *This* is what makes goroutines so intriguing.

Conclusion

We've now traversed the entire landscape of concurrency in Go: from first principles, to basic usage, to patterns, and how the runtime does things. I sincerely hope this book has given you a good grasp of concurrency in Go and aids you in completing all your glorious hacks. Thank you!

Appendix

As you set forth on your journey of writing concurrent code, you'll need the tools to write your program and analyze it for correctness, and a few helpful pointers to help you understand what's happening within your programs. Lucky for you, the Go ecosystem has a rich set of tooling both from the Go team and from the community! This appendix will discuss some of these tools and how they can aid you before, during, and after development. Since this book is focused on concurrency, I'm going to constrain the conversation to only topics that help you write or analyze concurrent code. We'll also briefly look at what happens when goroutines panic. It doesn't happen often, but the output can be a bit confusing the first time you see it.

Anatomy of a Goroutine Error

It happens to the best of us: sooner or later, your program will panic. If you're lucky, no humans or computers will be harmed in the process, and the worst that will happen is you'll be staring down the bad end of a stack trace.

Prior to Go 1.6, when a goroutine panicked, the runtime would print stack traces of all the currently executing goroutines. Sometimes this made it difficult (or at least time-consuming) to determine what had happened. At the time of this writing, Go 1.6 and greater greatly simplify things by printing only the stack trace of the panicking goroutine.

For example, when this simple program is executed:

```
1 package main
2
3 func main() {
4     waitForever := make(chan interface{})
5     go func() {
6         panic("test panic")
7     }()
8     <-waitForever
9 }
```

The following stack trace is produced:

```
panic: test panic

goroutine 4 [running]:
main.main.func1() ❸
    /tmp/babel-3271QbD/go-src-32713Rn.go:6 +0x65 ❶
created by main.main
    /tmp/babel-3271QbD/go-src-32713Rn.go:7 +0x4e ❷
exit status 2
```

❶   Refers to where the panic occurred.

❷   Refers to where the goroutine was started.

❸   Indicates the name of the function running as a goroutine. If it's an anonymous function as in this example, an automatic and unique identifier is assigned.

If you'd like to see the stack traces of all the goroutines that were executing when the program panicked, you can enable the old behavior by setting the GOTRACEBACK environmental variable to all.

Race Detection

In Go 1.1, a -race flag was added as a flag for most go commands:

```
$ go test -race mypkg     # test the package
$ go run -race mysrc.go   # compile and run the program
$ go build -race mycmd    # build the command
$ go install -race mypkg  # install the package
```

If you're a developer and all you need is a more reliable way to detect race conditions, this is really all you need to know. One caveat of using the race detector is that the algorithm will only find races that are contained in code that is exercised. For this reason, the Go team recommends running a build of your application built with the race flag under real-world load. This increases the probability of finding races by virtue of increasing the probability that more code is exercised.

There are also some options you can specify via environmental variables to tweak the behavior of the race detector, although generally the defaults are sufficient:

LOG_PATH
This tells the race detector to write reports to the *LOG_PATH.pid* file. You can also pass it special values: stdout and stderr. The default value is stderr.

STRIP_PATH_PREFIX
This tells the race detector to strip the beginnings of file paths in reports to make them more concise.

HISTORY_SIZE

This sets the per-goroutine history size, which controls how many previous memory accesses are remembered per goroutine. The valid range of values is [0, 7]. The memory allocated for goroutine history begins at 32 KB when HISTORY_SIZE is 0, and doubles with each subsequent value for a maximum of 4 MB at a HISTORY_SIZE of 7. When you see "failed to restore the stack" in reports, that's an indicator to increase this value; however, it can significantly increase memory consumption.

Given this simple program we first looked at in Chapter 1:

```
1 var data int
2 go func() { ❶
3     data++
4 }()
5 if data == 0 {
6     fmt.Printf("the value is %v.\n", data)
7 }
```

You would receive this error:

```
==================
WARNING: DATA RACE
Write by goroutine 6:
  main.main.func1()
      /tmp/babel-10285ejY/go-src-10285GUP.go:6 +0x44  ❶

Previous read by main goroutine:
  main.main()
      /tmp/babel-10285ejY/go-src-10285GUP.go:7 +0x8e  ❷

Goroutine 6 (running) created at:
  main.main()
      /tmp/babel-10285ejY/go-src-10285GUP.go:6 +0x80
==================
Found 1 data race(s)
exit status 66
```

❶ Signifies a goroutine that is attempting to write unsynchronized memory access.

❷ Signifies a goroutine (in this case the main goroutine) trying to read this same memory.

The race detector is an extremely useful tool for automatically detecting race conditions in your code. I highly recommend integrating it as part of your continuous integration process. Again, because the race detection can only detect races that occur, and we covered how race conditions are sometime tricky to trigger, it should be continuously running real-world scenarios in an attempt to trigger one.

pprof

In large codebases, it can sometimes be difficult to ascertain how your program is performing at runtime. How many goroutines are running? Are your CPUs being fully utilized? How's memory usage doing? Profiling is a great way to answer these questions, and Go has a package in the standard library to support a profiler named "pprof."

pprof is a tool that was created at Google and can display profile data either while a program is running, or by consuming saved runtime statistics. The usage of the program is pretty well described by its help flag, so instead we'll stick to discussing the runtime/pprof package here—specifically as it pertains to concurrency.

The runtime/pprof package is pretty simple, and has predefined profiles to hook into and display:

```
goroutine    - stack traces of all current goroutines
heap         - a sampling of all heap allocations
threadcreate - stack traces that led to the creation of new OS threads
block        - stack traces that led to blocking on synchronization primitives
mutex        - stack traces of holders of contended mutexes
```

From the context of concurrency, most of these are useful for understanding what's happening within your running program. For example, here's a goroutine that can help you detect goroutine leaks:

```
log.SetFlags(log.Ltime | log.LUTC)
log.SetOutput(os.Stdout)

// Every second, log how many goroutines are currently running.
go func() {
    goroutines := pprof.Lookup("goroutine")
    for range time.Tick(1*time.Second) {
        log.Printf("goroutine count: %d\n", goroutines.Count())
    }
}()

// Create some goroutines which will never exit.
var blockForever chan struct{}
for i := 0; i < 10; i++ {
    go func() { <-blockForever }()
    time.Sleep(500*time.Millisecond)
}
```

These built-in profiles can really help you profile and diagnose issues with your program, but of course you can write custom profiles tailored to help you monitor your programs:

```go
func newProfIfNotDef(name string) *pprof.Profile {
    prof := pprof.Lookup(name)
    if prof == nil {
        prof = pprof.NewProfile(name)
    }
    return prof
}

prof := newProfIfNotDef("my_package_namespace")
```

Index

W

wait for condition, 12
WaitGroup, 47
web scale, 3

work cancellation, 90, 155
  (see also timeouts and cancellations)
work stealing strategy, 197-212

About the Author

Katherine Cox-Buday is a computer scientist currently working at Simple. Her hobbies include software engineering, creative writing, Go (igo, baduk, weiquei), and music, all of which she pursues intermittently and with various levels of dedication.

Colophon

The animal on the cover of *Concurrency in Go* is the short-eared elephant shrew (*Macroscelides proboscideus*), a small mammal native to arid regions of Namibia, Botswana, and South Africa. Also known as a sengi, short-eared elephant shrews get their name from their elongated snout, which is thought to resemble an elephant's trunk.

Short-eared elephant shrews weigh between 28 and 43 grams and can grow to 10 centimeters in length, making them the smallest species in the elephant shrew family. Their fur is brown and gray with a white underbelly. They feed on insects like termites, ants, and worms, as well as plants like berries and leaf shoots.

Although short-eared elephant shrews are mainly solitary, they are one of the few mammals to mate monogamously. Mating pairs will team up to defend their territory from other shrews. The lifespan of a short-eared elephant shrew is one to two years in the wild, but they have been shown to live up to four years in captivity.

Many of the animals on O'Reilly covers are endangered; all of them are important to the world. To learn more about how you can help, go to *animals.oreilly.com*.

The cover image is from *Braukhaus Lexicon*. The cover fonts are URW Typewriter and Guardian Sans. The text font is Adobe Minion Pro; the heading font is Adobe Myriad Condensed; and the code font is Dalton Maag's Ubuntu Mono.

Learn from experts.
Find the answers you need.

Sign up for a **10-day free trial** to get **unlimited access** to all of the content on Safari, including Learning Paths, interactive tutorials, and curated playlists that draw from thousands of ebooks and training videos on a wide range of topics, including data, design, DevOps, management, business—and much more.

Start your free trial at:

oreilly.com/safari

(No credit card required.)